D0927851

18

BOOKSHOPS

18 BOOKSHOPS

Anne Scott

First published in Great Britain by
SANDSTONE PRESS LTD
PO BOX 5725
ONE HIGH STREET
DINGWALL
ROSS-SHIRE
IV15 9WJ
SCOTLAND

www.sandstonepress.com

Editor: Robert Davidson

ISBN: 978-1-905207-71-8

Sandstone Press is committed to a sustainable future in publishing, marrying the needs of the company and our readers with those of the wider environment. This book is made from paper certified by the Forest Stewardship Council.

Book design by
JULES AKEL, DALWHINNIE

Printed and bound in Poland.

Acknowledgements & Dedication

The author and publisher gratefully acknowledge the quotations which have been utilised in 18 Bookshops.

In the chapter on LEAKEY'S BOOKSHOP, INVERNESS, the lines beginning 'The end of all our exploring . . .' are from *Little Gidding* by T. S. Eliot, and come from *The Complete Poems and Plays of T. S. Eliot* published by Faber & Faber Ltd, London in 1969.

In the chapter on BOOKS OF WONDER, NEW YORK CITY, the discourse beginning 'So it's true', he thought . . .' are from *The Mysteries of Harris Burdick* by Chris van Allsburg published by Houghton Mifflin Harcourt Publishing Company, Boston in 1984.

In the chapter on BAUERMEISTER'S BOOKSHOP, EDINBURGH, the lines beginning 'So I give her this month . . .' and later 'So that if now . . .' are from *Autumn Journal* by Louis MacNeice published by Faber & Faber Ltd, London in 1939.

In the chapter on THE ATLANTIS BOOKSHOP, LONDON, the lines 'passing moments in a single day' and 'miraculous, the exercises in attention and observations' are from *In Search of the Miraculous: Fragments of an Unknown Teaching* by Piotr Ouspensky published by Routledge, London in 1949.

In the chapter on CARRAROE, CONNEMARA, the poem *Dwelling Place* is original, by the book's author, Anne Scott.

The principle of fair dealing has been observed throughout.

❧

THANKS ESPECIALLY TO MIKE SCOTT AND MICHAEL HAWKINS.

CONTENTS

FIRST...

FOR A YEAR OR TWO WHEN I WAS A CHILD, MY OLDER BROTHER BOUGHT A PENGUIN BOOK EACH SATURDAY MORNING, AND HE TOOK ME WITH him. The bookshop he liked was curved inside like a longboat, with the Penguins up in the bows ranged out in the stripes of their covers, white with orange, pink, green, dark blue.

Green Saturdays meant he was on holiday and reading mysteries: pink, he wanted to be travelling in the Kalahari, to Marrakesh, the South Seas: dark blue meant people's lives, orange was stories. The Penguins were flat like chocolate bars, and perfect to touch. He collected hardcover books too—bought without me—shining narrow volumes about drawing, and after a while we had to go to Crawford's second-hand furniture room to buy a book-case, carefully searching out the kind with shelves at different levels.

One Saturday a few weeks later, as we walked through the town, I saw an empty orange-box outside Horne's grocery: slender cream wood with a broad middle spar and a picture of bright oranges on the top.

'Look!' I whispered to him. 'Shelves!'

'Go on in,' he said. 'See if he'll give it to you.'

He did and we took it home. By evening my few books were in: my school bible, my red dictionary, *Grey Owl, Robinson Crusoe,* and my annuals laid flat on the low shelf.

The first books I owned smelt all their lives of tangerines.

The next week in our bookshop my brother bought a paperback for me too, my choice, *The Family from One End Street* by Eve Garnett. The bookseller made me a present of a bookmark with a red cord and placed it in at page one. Then we all went up into the bows of the longboat to buy my brother's Penguin.

I think this book was born that day.

I

COMPENDIUM BOOKSHOP
CAMDEN

The Spread Sail

In the summer of 1968 in an Edinburgh bookshop I discovered a guidebook by a born Londoner and new spy storywriter, Len Deighton. This was *London Dossier,* designed for someone who needed to know how to have a week in London on very little money, culturally well and as safely as possible. Me.

I wintered it into my head and in 1969, about the time the Woodstock Festival was tuning up, set off south with my ten-year-old son in a two-berth sleeper from Waverley Station. I booked us into The Mount Pleasant Hotel and we took London into our lives.

Map in hand, he mastered the Tube system and we rode south to the River, circled to the centre for music magazines and records, and one day followed Len Deighton on the Northern Line to Marine Ices in Chalk Farm—I still feel the thrill in the words—and that evening we crossed the road from there to see Nicol Williamson as Hamlet at The Roundhouse.

The *Dossier* became a second adult in our plans and if it had been written a year later, it would surely have shown us the way to *Compendium Books,* a new, unique, and never-matched marvel of shelves and titles, opened first in 1968 at 240 Camden High Street, extended in 1972 to include number 281, and then consolidated at 234 where I found it at last in the summer of 1975.

It had been open only some weeks. Work to do with wood was still in progress. The shop smelt of its pine shelves shining white. The books were fat and thin, bright-sleeved, very tempting to touch. I thought I knew books but there were so many strangers here, whole streets of foreign covers and names, philosophers I had never read, Portuguese poets, African novelists. As the Franco dictatorship drew to a close, Miguel Hernandez poetry was here on the shelves and Federico Garcia Lorca's *Blood Wedding, The House of Bernarda Alba*; Latin Americans Pablo Neruda, and Jorge Luis Borges whom I knew only as an inspiration to James Kennaway writing novels in Scotland a decade before. The aisles were lined with esoteric books and Ann Shepherd was assembling what was the first big collection of Mind and Spirit books in Britain.

I wish I had been in at the start back in 1968 when Nick Kimberley was building the poetry sections with authors far and far beyond the reach of other bookshops. Now in 1975 he was bringing them here: the New York poets—Frank O'Hara (whom somehow I missed until I found his poems much later in New York), John Ashbery, Charles Olsen: San Francisco editions from the City Lights Bookshop, Lawrence Ferlinghetti, Allen Ginsberg's *Howl,* Jack Kerouac's *On the Road,* of course, but also his poetry and a copy of *Trip-Trap,* the book of Haiku he wrote at Thanksgiving in 1959 on another road journey, from San Francisco to Long Island to visit his mother.

Jack Kerouac had, contained in himself, the qualities I found in Compendium. He was unexpected, he could be rhapsodic or hard in his tastes. He revered writing and he was not afraid to run against grains and assumptions. His biographer and friend Ann Charters flew over to speak in Compendium about the Beats and Frank O'Hara. Later, Brian Patten and other Liverpool poets giving readings in the shop, thanked the New York writers for their courage as new released voices. I could find their books nowhere else with such ease.

There was also the sheer knowledge in the shop. The staff members were expert each in a personal field. They could give you a small seminar on your writer and find the book or collection you most needed. Some of their stock, their attitudes, their dreams had been visualised and set out in *The Dialectics of Liberation Conference* that had been held at The Roundhouse in 1967: their books were not ever to be confined by mainstream traditions or expectations or accepted conformities.

Compendium introduced me to *The Colour Purple* by Alice Walker, *I Know Why the Caged Bird Sings* by Maya Angelou, Peter de Vries's *Comfort Me with Apples* and Jerome Salinger's *Raise High the Roofbeam, Carpenters,* through the enthusiasm of a cheerful American book-woman.

In the seventies and early eighties my brother and then my son moved to London and so my times of being there increased. Work sent me on a long weekend each spring and altogether I fell in love with London. I became a member of the Penn Club in Bedford Place so as to wake each morning above trees in a Bloomsbury square and be near Covent Garden and the outdoor cafés.

A fellow Scot named Mike Hart arrived to work at Compendium in 1982. On my visits across the next decade, he turned my reading to Tom Leonard, James Kelman, Alastair Gray's *Lanark,* and a closer understanding of James Kennaway's novels. These were all Scottish and easily bought at home: but at Compendium Mike would take a book in his hand, turn it over and think, then open it fast at a page, and read from it, so swift and clean and quiet that I heard the words straight from the writer's mind, the pretences of paper and print exactly gone. A paragraph, a stanza, and he would finish, leave the book open at the place, and go away. It was done in a minute or two, an orchestration of word and voice and time and place. I had never seen such open thinking with the mind playing on the words. What James Boswell caught in Samuel Johnson.

In 1986, I went to America for the first time, to take part in book-events at Ann Arbor and in Kansas City. A friend I made bought me a very American present—a 'book bag', my first, with a stars-and-stripes address tag and a long zipper—to carry my American books back to Britain.

Writers were generous with their work: Robert Cormier gave me *The Chocolate War* and the theosophist John Algeo his work-in-progress on the earliest *A Wizard of Oz.* I would not, they told me, 'likely find these in London book houses', but by then Compendium had complete ranges of Cormier and reprinted rare copies of Frank Baum.

Of the books I bought there, I still have, in casual count, work by Walt Whitman, Maya Angelou, a dignified Thames and Hudson *Henry James and His World,* Elizabeth Bishop, Emily Dickinson, and others so assimilated as 'my books' that now I can't see them. I wish Mike Hart had talked to me about Frank O'Hara whose urban life-transforming poetry I found, on a day in Greenwich Village with my son, in 1992. By the time I was buying his poetry widely, and finding his art criticism and the biographies of him, it was 2001 and Compendium Books had just closed: and a year later, Mike Hart died. The old shops in the High Street, the single traders, had vanished too, the ones with

Fruiterer, Ironmonger, Baker, Fish, inscribed across the windows.

What stays with me now is not only the books I bought in Compendium but how its being, and its men and women, showed me that bookshops are immeasurably strange and that the mind reading next to mine inhabits a separate earth. What people saw from the street was a glass door always open and wide windows shelved with outfacing books. I remember how hardworking the street was: rough underfoot, busy with purposes, loading, shifting, getting started, getting on. Inside the shop were encounters with hard-working men and women, ready intelligence, habitual discovery.

And help, always help. 'Do you have?' I would ask and follow the sure stepping bookman through the sweet-pine shelving. Growing accustomed to this company, to the light in the eyes, I knew the shape and order of this place in my life.

Imago Mundi.

I

THE SPREAD SAIL

2

CHEPMAN AND MYLLAR
EDINBURGH
1507–1510

Three Years' Light

THE KING WAS BEHIND IT, OF COURSE, THIS WHOLE PLAN FOR A PRINTING PRESS IN EDINBURGH, KING JAMES IV, RENAISSANCE PRINCE, designer, soldier, linguist, scholar, noble mind. Shakespeare may have patterned the soul of Hamlet on him, this northern universal man who died, in the end, of a kinsman's promises.

In 1507 his country was vibrant. Two years before, he had granted a Charter to the Royal College of Surgeons when the Barber Surgeons of Edinburgh were formally incorporated as a Craft Guild. There were three universities—St Andrews, Aberdeen, and Glasgow. He had married the daughter of his ally Henry VII of

England, and he had just commissioned the world's greatest ship to be built at Newhaven.

It would be *The Great Michael*, named for the Archangel and signifying by 1511 the foundation of a master navy in Europe. James was, as well, a patron of artists and musicians, he recommended archery to the citizens for fitness and grace and self defence. He valued books and collected a library of both manuscripts from all over Europe, and printed works from France, bound in vellum, reindeer hide, velvet lettered in gold. He was himself a negotiator and diplomat, recruiting young men of proven integrity and skill to serve in the Office of the King's Secretary as letter-writers whose work appeared above the King's signature and seal—Writers to the Signet.

Among them from 1494 was Walter Chepman, the same age, 21, as James, and already a merchant trading across Europe in wood for shipbuilding, in wool, velvets and damasks. By 1507, when he was called into royal service, he was ready to realise the King's command for a National Printing Press in Edinburgh. While he looked forward to his own entrepreneurial work and financial interest in the new enterprise, Chepman first needed to find a colleague, a man with supreme publishing and printing expertise, and he turned to Andro Myllar, an Edinburgh bookseller who had already supplied the King with books printed abroad, possibly in Rouen where Scots authors traditionally had their work printed, and where Myllar had himself been trained into the printing trade.

He had been a bookseller in Edinburgh for years, travelling to France and Germany for printed books. There were many to choose from. By 1497, the Archbishop of St Andrews had a library of more than twenty foreign imports. Scottish authors sent their manuscripts abroad for printing: Andro Myllar and others brought them home for selling.

They varied in subject. James Liddell's philosophical writings from the University of Paris where he taught may have been, in 1495, the earliest printed Scottish work to be imported. By 1505 we hear of Andro Myllar—*andreas myllar scotus*—setting out his requirements for art and diligence in the making and correcting of two books, a grammarian work and an elucidation of a Missal, which he had commissioned for publishing with the Rouen printing house. His instructions demanded of the French craftsmen the accuracy and high skill he had himself, and his dedication. Reputation was everything. He made it known to his customers and book-collectors that in his absences to Rouen, his wife would receive commissions and ensure their safe keeping against his return. His personal device—a miller on a ladder—was his promise and seal on a book's perfection. Geoffrey Chaucer would have admired him: he is in the fourteenth century tradition of excellent public man.

Late in 1507 he arranged for a Printing Press to come from France: by sea to the east coast of Scotland and then by carriage and cart to Edinburgh. For such a new and hazardous journey, the metal types would be packed in wood chests, oil-based inks sealed in jars, the parts and plates of the Press itself cosseted and saved in cloth and chested too. Foreign printers travelled with it and perhaps also Myllar himself, seeing the venture through. Finally it all came home and was set up in a workshop prepared by Chepman in the Southgait in Edinburgh, at the end of Blackfriars Wynd off the Canongate.

On 15th September 1507, King James delivered Letters Patent to Masters Chepman and Myllar to inaugurate them officially as Printers to His Majesty. The Letters acknowledge that our 'lovattis servitouris Walter Chepman and Andro Myllar has takin on thame to furnish and bring hame ane prent, with al stuff belangand therto, and expert men to use the samyne for imprenting within our Realme of the bukis of our Lawis, actis of parliament, croniclis, mess bukis and portuus efter the use of our Realme'... The King also undertook to make a grant, possibly with Chepman's help, to finance the Press and the bookselling.

The most telling words in the Letters Patent are those about the mess bukis and portuus — Mass Books and Breviaries — further emphasised later where they are to be 'usit generally within al our Realme alssone as the samynn may be prentit and providit, and that na maner of sic bukis of Salusbery use be brocht to be sauld within our Realme in tym cuming'.

The emphasis explains the King's urgency to have a Press in Scotland at this time when the Scots form of the Mass was being, as he saw it, infiltrated with English forms unacceptable to Scottish worship, and particularly offensive to the powerful William Elphinstone, Bishop of Aberdeen and adviser to King James, who had his own *Scots Breviary* ready for printing. Seen in this light, the Edinburgh Printing Press was a national instrument of religious defence.

What false beginnings followed, what hard winter days and rough exchanges between Scot and Frenchman? What sweating anxieties in Myllar and Chepman? We can never know. But by the fourth day of aperile the yhere of God MCCCCC and viii yheris—4th April 1508—they had ready the first dated printed book in Scotland. This was a long poem by John Lydgate, a Romance work named *The Maying or Disport of Chaucer Or The Complaint of the Black Knight.*

Over the next months, nine separate booklets making up a series of poems and prose pieces, came off the Press, 216 pages in all, new-printed. There were poems by William Dunbar and by Robert Henryson, Romance verse and lyrical poetry and a piece of prose. Each book was six inches tall, fit for the hand so that a reader might carry Henryson's *Orpheus and Eurydice,* Dunbar's *Golden Targe* and *The Twa Merrit Wemen and The Wedow* into gardens, where Readings took place and short dramatisations, to make time pass in carriages on journeys, into daily reading life. Reading as a solitary pleasure evolved. Where manuscripts had been too fragile to go, bound books were safe, and so Scots poetry was brought easily to the table as well as to the mind. The printed works cost less in time and money than manuscripts and were cheaper than French imports. Small personal collections began. Best of all, bookshops spread.

Perhaps the poems were test-runs for the press, and first tries for the printers, as some historians have argued, though there is no real evidence: but I believe Chepman and Myllar saw how their Press would spread the names of Scots poets through the two kingdoms as William Caxton's printing of Chaucer's *Canterbury Tales* had spread his name. William Dunbar was already a Court poet, Robert Henryson writing in Dunfermline, was still to be acknowledged as a poet surpassing Dunbar, perhaps even Geoffrey Chaucer himself. But that accolade comes later, in the twentieth century.

All the work of that year 1508–09 survives in only one single set of the poetry—the nine Chepman and Myllar Prints in The National Library of Scotland. *The Scottish Breviary of The Mass* was duly and successfully printed for Bishop Elphinstone and King James in late 1509 or early 1510.

And then there was no more from the Press. Andro Myllar was not heard of after 1513 and only Chepman's name appeared on the Breviary. King James IV was killed at the battle of Flodden in 1513. His Renaissance Court at Holyrood declined and, with it, potential patronage for literature. His son, crowned James V, was a child: the Regency ensured he had no instrumental powers for seventeen years. In 1528 after a full and rewarded merchant's life Walter Chepman died without any further reference to his amazing enterprise of 1507–1510.

When in 1532 King James V revived the office of King's Printer, Thomas Davidson from Birse in Aberdeenshire, now printer in the High Street of Edinburgh, was admittit to his heines prenntare. Ten years later, the King gave him premises for printing and bookselling 'on the North side of the High Street', in a house where Walter Chepman too had lived.

David Chepman, Walter's son, set up as Bookbinder in Edinburgh from 1526 to 1541 and had court business too. In 1539 he bound and laid about with gold, a matin buik for the Queen.

But of the great Press of 1508 and the Southgait printing bookshop, nothing is heard. It too had been a King's servant, servitour to his duty as the Stewart defender of the Scottish Mass.

Yet James IV had not foreseen, as his printers had done, that the first pieces from his Press, the poems, would be its greater work: and that they would send the names of William Dunbar and Robert Henryson to booksellers across Europe and into the mainstream of Renaissance writing. In 1604, 1605 and 1607 the Edinburgh publishing firm of Charteris brought out reprints of Henryson's *The Testament of Cresseid*, for by then English lawyers and diplomats were using the poem to teach themselves Middle Scots, and Scottish ways, now that they had to serve a Scottish King, James VI and I, great grandson to James IV.

3

THE PARROT
ST PAUL'S CHURCHYARD, LONDON
1609

These to be Solde by Wm Aspley at His Shop

WHEN WILLIAM ASPLEY OPENED OUT THE SHUTTERS OF THE PARROT, HIS NEW BOOKSHOP, IN 1608, HE HAD NO VISION OF THE momentous event he would stage there in the following spring. Already thirty bookshops traded for business in Paul's Churchyard, crowded over a place of ancient burial. Aspley shared an inner wall with his neighbour to the east, Thomas Clarke at The Angel: and a narrow alley on the west side with Edward Bishop, trading at the long-fronted spacious Brazen Serpent.

The shop signs of this community of booksellers sped like flags along the Yard, brilliant in colour and design—The Ball, The

Fleur de Lys, The Golden Lion, The Green Dragon, The White Greyhound, Holy Lamb, Peacock, Pigeon, Phoenix . . . A man could take his sign with him to his next shop and hang it there, as Francis Eglesfield did in 1642, moving with his Marigold blazon when he shifted three shops east. No two bookshops were alike. They differed in their size inside and on their pavement fronts. The King's Arms had most space: it was almost 28 feet square as far as I can measure from the map drawn after the Great Fire in 1666 revealed the foundations.

The Parrot had some 18 feet to the front with a depth of about 23 feet. It seems not to have had storeyed accommodation above. Some of the Yard shops were in substantial tall houses and traded upward from at least the ground floor. Wherever possible, as at The Parrot, a good space was laid out with a book-table and chairs along the shelves.

Outside, a sloping board—the stall-board—hung protectively above the window, supported by struts to the street or to the shop wall: sometimes this would be over-reached by a further little roof, the penthouse or 'pentice'. By contrast, a 'shedde' was essentially a stall with its stall-board and pentice hinged to act as enclosing shutters for the books inside, a structure close-kin to the 'lucken-booths', the locking booths, in Edinburgh.

By 1600, both shops and sheddes were permanent on their sites, but in the 14th and 15th centuries, manuscripts, paper scrolls, handwritten almanacs and prayers were publicly sold by 'stationers' from their 'stations', portable fold-up booths and stalls ready to be whipped shut and carried to whatever space had a surge of likely customers gathering—scriveners, clerics, clerks, amanuenses. As those were just the kind of buyers to be found near St Paul's Old Church, the Yard had early become a recognised trading place for readers. A fine place, as William Aspley knew, to be opening a shop in 1608.

The Parrot was his second shop, coming after he had traded for some years at The Tiger's Head, a smaller place he could still see across the Yard, beyond The Ball and The Fleur de Lys. His new shop was shorter to the front, but deeper by far, allowing for more stock-space and ease for customers. He was now better placed.

He had been noticed early in the trade. When he turned fourteen in the Christmas of 1587, he was selected Apprentice by George Bishop, a distinguished publisher newly assigned to the full management of the Queen's Printing House. Nine years of strict apprenticeship later, Aspley, at twenty-three, was received into the Mastership of his trade and twelve months after that, to the status of Freeman of The Stationers' Company. This was a fast rise. In 1608, an experienced bookman about to open at The Parrot, Aspley was a figure to observe.

The Parrot had had four tenants since 1576 but now in 1608 its life stabilised and became one with its new man. For the following thirty years, he would make this Bookshop his life. Over his counter, from his table, out of the displays on Saint Paul's Yard, he would sell unprecedented books making their entrance into The Renaissance, into London, into time itself.

He brought an expertise in play publishing. At The Tiger's Head he had published and sold William Shakespeare's *Henry IV Part II* and *Much Ado About Nothing* new-printed for him in Quarto form, as accurate as any quarto from its time, there being apparently no proven authenticated scripts coming from Shakespeare himself.

By this move, he established himself as publisher, bookseller and a trader habitual to commissioning a printer. In 1603 he was selling copies of speeches given before the new King, James I and VI, an enterprise diplomatic, and competitively done by commissioning his printer fast to do a careful work entitled *Speeches Delivered To The King's Most Excellent Majesty in The Name of The Sheriffs of London and Middlesex.*

Six years on in 1609, Robert Waldegrave, printer in Edinburgh to The King's Most Excellent Majestie, petitioned Aspley for the right to reprint the speeches. By then Aspley was at The Parrot and his note of agreement would go out from there. In 1609, too, he began issuing a Catalogue for customers, a certain sign of a more spacious shop, an extended stock and a name getting known.

Whatever he had to sell, Shakespeare could have bought. Did he come into The Parrot for William Strachey's startling success *The True Repertory of The Wreck*, and to look at other accounts of the marvellous adventure just happened in Bermuda, and so begin the dream that would emerge into *The Tempest* in 1610? He had surely purchased his books widely in Paul's Yard: not his own plays, perhaps, in misheard, misprinted quartos, but treatises *On Melancholy*, and John Florio's 1603 translation of Michel de Montaigne's essays on *Love and Friendship*, and Francis Bacon's early 1597 essays: Lucius Plutarch's *Lives* in Thomas North's translation in 1597, Ralph Holinshed's *Chronicles* two years earlier, *The Prince* by Niccolo Machiavelli, *The Courtier*, Baldassare Castiliogne's manual for ambitious diplomats, Edmund Spenser, Philip Sidney, Christopher Marlowe: the new dramatists Cyril Tourneur and Thomas Dekker—was Shakespeare there to buy those, all set out on tables for him?

But he was at home in Stratford in May 1609 when William Aspley began to sell, under his own imprint, his four hundred copies of *The Sonnets*, riskily new and tensely perfect presented as—

Shakespeare's Sonnets Never before Imprinted
At London by G. Eld for Thomas Thorpe
To Be Solde by William Aspley

What happened that spring day? Did the customers in The Parrot ask the questions that have crowded round *The Sonnets* for centuries? Did Thomas Thorpe have the rights to the poems when he published the Quarto? Had Shakespeare agreed and did he sell the work directly to Thorpe, whose name was good in that year when he had successfully published Ben Jonson and John Marston? Who was this 'Onlie Begetter' with no name, shadowing the title page? Why had Shakespeare left the poems undedicated? Who had chosen 'The Parrot'? Aspley could tell us, but if he answered in 1609, we have not heard him these four hundred years. A brother bookman William (or John) Wright sold the other half of the First Quarto print run under his own imprint from his shop at Christ Church Gate near Newgate.

Many of Aspley's copies would be stitched, not bound, so that the buyer might choose his leather and lettering—red half Morocco with a gold frame line and lettering perhaps: or he could take them as they were, in leaf. Edward Alleyn, the star actor at Philip Henslowe's Curtein Theatre, bought his Sonnets at The Parrot on 19th June and paid five pence before the binding. Four of the Aspley imprints exist still, living into their fifth century under glass in The British Library, The Bodleian Library Oxford, The Huntingdon Library, San Marino, California, and The Folger Shakespeare Library in Washington D.C.

Aspley secured his name at 'Parrot' with this beginning. He became a publisher of further Shakespeare quartos, and in 1623 was confirmed as member of the Syndicate formed to bring out The First Folio, the Shakespeare canon, the plays gathered into the only accredited version of the best texts by John Hemynge and Francis Condell. In 1640, the year he died, he was splendidly elected to be Master of The Stationers' Company.

He had endured long, through the execution in 1618 of Walter Raleigh whose poetry was on his shelves, and then in 1625 the death of King James who had signed the death warrant. With his bookman's imagination, he saw how language and books were transformed by *The Authorised Version of The Bible* in 1611—The King James *Bible*—with Shakespeare still alive to hear it. In the new reign of Charles I, when John Donne's son published his father's poems in 1633, Aspley would have them. In 1637, there would be John Milton and *Lycidas* a new poet and a new poetry, a lifetime away from the spirit of *The Sonnets* of 1609. A bookshop's lifetime too. The Parrot's walls had sheltered the most transformative writers in the language, men who transfigured thinking itself.

In 1640 Aspley conveyed his lease to Luke Fawne who left The Brazen Serpent for The Parrot and kept it for twenty-six years. What was there for him to set out on the old shelves? Henry Vaughan's metaphysical and divine poetry in 1646, Izaak Walton's *Compleat Angler* in 1655, John Harrington's vision of a utopian republic, *The Commonwealth of Oceania* in 1656, lyric innovations by Robert Herrick and Richard Lovelace in 1648.

The Parrot would have adapted its window display to the emergence of political writing and the new, great prose appearing now: in 1644 John Milton's *Areopagitica,* his great argument for freedom of the press, and during the Cromwell Protectorate, *Leviathan,* Thomas Hobbes's scrutiny of sovereignty published in 1651 to a readership still shocked and divided by the execution of Charles I in 1649. The Parrot survived into the Restoration of 1660 and it may be that in that year Luke Fawne was seeing his customers changing in their tastes and needs. Possibly they were less scholarly and younger than Aspley had known, and now more varied as money for books spread more accessibly through the classes.

Browsers in 'Parrot' would find the first popular satirical prose in the new voice of Samuel Butler. His *Hudibras* came out in two volumes in 1662 and 1663, sharp with modern scepticism and an ambiguous tone. Connected with this new direct critical purpose of literature are the beginnings of literary criticism as a genre in writing and as a source of reputation.

The Parrot would have John Bunyan's books on the table too: not yet *The Pilgrim's Progress,* but *The Holy City* in 1662 and *Grace Abounding* in 1663. There would be Edmund Spenser and John Donne, being bought and read again for what they had once written about change, mutability, mortality: Thomas Browne's poetry for the same reason.

The Bookshops of Paul's Yard struggled through the Plague of 1665. After The Great Fire in 1666, nothing is heard again of The Parrot. It disappears with all its books, all its neighbours and all their signs.

But in the rebuilding of St Paul's Yard, as Christopher Wren's Cathedral rises alongside, the little shop comes alive again. Its foundations now merged with The Angel next door, it opens for bookselling as The Rose and Crown. I should put 'it seems probable' in that sentence, but I don't want to. There is a new bookshop on the site. What else can it be but The Parrot miraculously returned?

THESE TO BE SOLDE BY WM ASPLEY
AT HIS SHOP

4

THE OLD PRINTING PRESS BOOKSHOP IONA

Reckoning

THIS IS A MONASTIC CELL WITH A BEAUTIFUL LOW DOOR AND A STEP, A SMALL WINDOW SET INTO ANCIENT DEEP STONES, THICK-WHITE with paint. Limewashed it would have been in its earlier life as a shelter for hired harvestmen homeless on the island. Daylight passes from the road into the window and falls on a dark embroidered cover, a single closed book and some brass pieces, a cross, candlesticks, and a folded standing note of opening times. On darkish days there is a lamp in there, a tiny glow along this pilgrim track that leads on to The Street of the Dead and The Abbey Church where scribes once wrote, candled and quilled to keep a light alive.

There are two small rooms inside, arched apart. In the first the bookseller sits at a table, reading. Cards are for sale, and some small painted nets for cross-stitching, elegant as bookmarks. The walls carry a few historical posters of boats — coracles, ferries, and, very beautiful, the sailing ships and steamships that stood out in Martyrs' Bay to take off emigrants from 1750. A close-printed sheet with the history of the bookshop is pinned on the wall but too high for me to read. A round table carries blue booklets about Mull and Iona, local maps.

It's right, of course, not to have widened this little place. Small light and space hallow it with so much quiet. People whisper at the shelves until the room feels like a scriptorium, in the right dimension, and divided in two by a wall of books. The bookshop — or bookhouse is better — has no attached neighbour. It is alone, white, thick, and curving inside. Who knows how it began?

Once its true work was to hand-print books when William Muir and John McCormick, local men, arrived eagerly to open The Iona Press because, they said, 'Iona was a great seat of learning once' and they dream they will 'revive something of the ancient glory'.

They began with handmade printings of William Blake, his apocalyptic coloured visions emerging into the white northern space. They brought out *Altus Prosator* in English for visitors, only yards from where Saint Columba had written it in Latin a thousand years before. They bordered the pages with black and white Celtic patterns and these were finished by islanders who painted in the colour, working into the dark after the day's long work, following the ancient crosses and circles with an art they had learned from *The Book of Kells*: and that Book was their own, begun on Iona but taken to Kells to find protection from invaders to Iona in the ninth century.

Did they name the colours to each other in Gaelic? What is the Gaelic for gamboge, rose madder, lapis lazuli? Words more musical even than those.

The Press made prayer sheets: there were so many prayers on the island, soft sounds printed. Sailors' prayers for the beginning of a voyage, children's prayers for the start of the day. Each year the type was reset to make a flurry of guidebooks for summer, for sails, for walks to take, wild flowers to find. Over five, six years of island time, the Press sped its sheets in a noise of writing: small unclear pictures, news, happy days out described for strangers. Then it ended as the men who dreamed its beginning parted and went into other work.

Not far away, in the Heritage Centre, the curator shows me sepia picture-postcards from the original Press, each one lifted out from a soft covering. These are revenants, bought, written, sent, and now returned home. They show brown days on Iona, mahogany land, pale grained sky, silken sails.

I take postcard number 484/6 into my hand. It is 'On the Coast of Iona' and is not of our world, but stilled, a shadow ship standing off-shore. The writer tells me it is Midsummer Day 1912 and that she has been to the silversmith's shop to buy a present—

The Keeper allowed you to take it and send the money on.
Along the road at the landing place, children were selling green marble pebbles.

The pebbles were roundels of marble quarried from a shoulder of pale green stone above the shore where Columba's vessel came in: the children polished them in the sea. Picture postcards have become as brilliant as acrylic art, but the summer guides to Iona still hold the vision of Muir and McCormick. They are filled with information and decorated with a small oval photograph of the landing place. The past island pauses for a moment in the photos and cards in its old shop.

The books on the inner room shelves are muted in brown, dark red, and green covers and I search for something to read in my room. John Galsworthy is there, John Buchan, Thomas Hardy, Aldous Huxley, Osbert and Edith Sitwell. Sea-maps of soundings lie on the table, depths darkening blue. Rich-bound botanical books are opened at sweeping coloured plates, their filmy coverings rising in the draught.

I find Matthew Arnold's poems, and Robert Browning's, Walter de la Mare, Hugh Walpole's novels: travel books on the desert lands, reference works about the geology of the island, all with fine tweedy-coloured layer drawings. The paper of these books is nineteenth century, early twentieth, heavy and lasting. I like, though, the slim volumes of wartime poets, printed on bible-thin paper in the Forties and bound in pale grey cloth with dark red lettering, and the one-act plays for short holiday concentration. Longer volumes in the outer room are memoirs, some military, many Scottish, stories of great heroism, of Scotland, of religious lives. Here are colourful dust jackets showing their authors backed by troop ships, maps, cathedrals, tents and pyramids.

There is so much stillness.

The bookseller at her table speaks little and that in a murmur. This seems right. With the Press gone all these years, and the books finely bound on their wooden shelves, what source of sound? Outside is wild enough: a wind coming off the white water streams low through the village. In here there is time, and time, and time again. Someone is writing a postcard. How little writing has changed its shape or what it says.

If there is often no book for me, something else must keep me here and bring me back. It is not the memory the building keeps of the Press it held. It is whatever has been brought to the space by the men who sheltered in this bothy, and by the tired hands that painted in the Celtic mysteries. I return to hear whatever dreams the emigrants left, the families I see in the dark photographs taken at the leaving, and I want to catch a sound of children and sailors singing prayers.

The floor at my feet is hard and may be one with the walls

and roof and there is an encirclement of minds too. William Blake is here and the postcard writer from Midsummer Day 1912, with Saint Columba, and the scribes. The books in their upright rows are an imitation of life beautifully shelved in order, an alphabet enclosure of choices, and life made readable: but they have no charge equal to meet this space and the brilliant light in the narrow door.

5

LEAKEY'S BOOKSHOP
INVERNESS

Little Gidding

LEAKEY'S DAZZLES IN A VAST DEMOCRATIC SPACE, LIGHT EVERYWHERE. LIKE EVERYONE ENTERING HERE FOR THE FIRST TIME, I KNEW ONE FACT — that its building by the river had been St Mary's Gaelic Church. How right this feels, for the Celtic Church is musical with words and the sound of voices carried away by them, and John Knox's white painted Reformed kirks were founded hard on differently heard words: on sermons articulated under headings in long, thought-through, exactly-punctuated sentences. Where better for books to assemble than here?

My first sight of the shop's interior made me think of a drawing I like, of Saint Paul's Yard in London in 1600 where an outdoor sermon is in progress. The high pulpit there is in this bookshop too, the banked up tiers of people in 1600 are here the books, row upon standing row, upward, tilting to each other like listeners.

To see all this is to remember the human link between churches and books. A bible was set out in every school and parish in Scotland after the Reformation. In part its purpose was to teach religious concepts but, far more thrillingly, it would teach reading to men and women and open for them all the worlds it leads to. In 1600 London, the churches and the new Globe playhouse sounded with intense rhythms, absorbing voices, spell-binding ideas. In this Northern place, they sang and read.

It's very quiet in the shop: or, more truthfully, it's very quiet up high in the shop. On the first floor and above there is a receding silence contained by the rafter roof, the arched windows: by the fine gold of the shining wood along the walls and by the gallery rail, and most of all by the poetry volumes on the shelves that run out into perspective. I see them up there and keep them for last. There is so much at hand to be seen, to be with, here on the ground floor.

Under the pulpit topped with books, there is a rectangular space walled with panels and opened by a little railed gate. Addressed packages are stacked on the floor. This is where a studious quiet bookseller is working, where we pay and where we ask for help. Payment is quick, efficient, not a scruple more than essential. Asking is different. The response comes after a pause and the words begin with 'we' in this shop. 'We have a copy—let me just show you where.' He points to the towers and lanes on our left and gives me an exact address. The book is there and in a minute is in my hand, an English-into-Gaelic dictionary.

The huge room is warm, wood-scented from a black stove standing in mid-floor, realised out of a folktale, in a forest of logs piled high on each side. Some of their brother woods will have gone to become books, or the paper that made the books. Further down the long floor, the black bellows of a spiral stair is climbing on bats' wing treads, iron like the stove. They lead to the pale gold gallery where I'm going, to the poetry shelves, the maps and the prints.

The Gaelic congregations who filled this high building before the books came sang in a language bearing twenty-eight separate words for 'poem'. In such a place I may find any poem, and from anywhere: from other lives too, since this is also a second-hand bookshop. There may be an early W. B. Yeats book first read in Dublin, one of the narrow perfect fine-paper volumes made by his sisters' Cuala Press, and I'm always looking for an 1855 New York copy of Walt Whitman's *Leaves of Grass.*

But high up on this shining bridge where I've never been before, I'm ready to believe I could find the dream unattainable—Shakespeare's Sonnets in the 1609 edition or the

1623 Folio of his plays, Wordsworth's first edition posthumous of *The Prelude* from 1850, and the 1633 John Donne. If anywhere, here, in the golden colour of this Klimt fall of books and light.

When I find it, the book I want is rare and plain. T. S. Eliot's *Little Gidding* finished and published in 1942, a war edition in cream card wraps with black lettered title. There are sixteen top-cut pages raw to the leading and lower edges, made from paper so dense and uneven it handles like early manuscript. The book is tall: octavo, nine inches by seven, slim and chaste. It is the last poem in the *Four Quartets* sequence, following *Burnt Norton, East Coker, The Dry Salvages,* and is the culmination of his work.

The first owner has signed himself on the opening page—

Charles R. Redwood, Richmond, July 1943
and then
Kneller School June 25th 1943

More than three hundred years before, in 1626, Nicholas Ferrar, newly created an Anglican Dean, left London with three generations of his family to establish a sanctuary Community in the small village of Little Gidding not far from Cambridge, with his brother John. He died there in 1637. Seventeen year-old Nicholas, John's son, succeeded with his father but died in 1640 just as the English Civil War was beginning. In the chaos months after Oliver Cromwell's final victory, John Ferrar gave sanctuary to the King,

Charles I, on his desperate ride north from Oxford to Scotland in May 1646, 'leading him over fields' in the dark.

The Community faded after 1657 when John Ferrar died: his great grandson restored the Church in 1714. In the two centuries before Eliot came in 1936 and 1942, it was a place of pilgrimage, and it is now. The Church and a small community house are there still to visit and stay in, alive in their history and in the poem I had found. There are celebrations of T. S. Eliot each November, readings of his work, and music.

Which of those twenty-eight Gaelic words for 'poem' is best for *Little Gidding*? *Dreacht* it might be—a pattern, its woven lines involving together London in the 1666 Great Fire and in its bombed blazing streets in 1940, both carrying 'death of hope, and despair' when the citizens watched their lives disappear. Or possibly *ambra*, being poem, dream and sword-hilt—words swirling and circling into a living design, carved images dissolving into shapes and visions, roses and flames infolded.

In the earlier *Quartets*, air, earth, and water—the elements of life—are celebrated, as they might have been here in this Inverness Church at Communion. But *Little Gidding* encompasses the element of fire, destructive but as well purifying a space and making a new place.

Best of all, *Little Gidding* is *uige*, ancient Gaelic in its believing that a poem is a precious stone, a deep-reflective jewel-place touched and renewed and shining, Eliot ending on the healing promise that—

The end of all our exploring
Will be to arrive where we started
And know the place for the first time.

Sometimes, as here, a Bookshop may be defined forever in a life by a single found book.

LITTLE GIDDING

5

6

WILLIAM TEMPLETON'S BOOKSHOP IRVINE 1782

The Crossing Place

6

IN 1782 WILLIAM TEMPLETON'S BOOKSHOP IN IRVINE OCCUPIED NARROW PREMISES IN THE HIGH STREET NEAR THE TOLBOOTH. THIS WAS A key area for local business and for passing trade, with strangers coming in by coach from Glasgow to the staging post across the road in the Glasgow Vennel.

By those same coaches Templeton imported books from the city and sent on parcels of new titles to merchants trading books to commissioning customers in Glasgow, Stirling, Edinburgh and Inverness. His connection with Ireland had been especially strong, a consistent and money-making trade in cheap reprints of

Dr Samuel Johnson's *Dictionary* and copies of his *Lives of the English Poets* from Dublin to the port of Irvine, but the heavy import tax brought a decline in the 1770s. By 1780 the Irish trade had gone underground, briskly successful as a smuggling line running from Dublin to Irvine and then north through Scotland. No tax or duty was paid, the books were illegal commerce but they sold widely: profit grew with demand. And besides, there was an edgy excitement to it for a North British bookman.

It had to stop. In 1781 the Custom Commissioners in Scotland, chaired on occasion by Adam Smith, set 'pursuers' to catch the captains of Irish boats with their cargoes at Irvine harbour. Riskily nearer to William Templeton, they searched and detained carriers at the Glasgow Vennel Weigh House across the road from his shop in full sight of his window.

No cadre of shipmasters was bringing in anti-clerical or seditious political inflammables. Their most carried author was always Samuel Johnson. Those copies of *The Lives of The English Poets,* a massive work commissioned in Tom Davies's bookshop in Covent Garden in 1779, were uncovered in a haul intercepted at Glasgow in 1781, the year of the final volume. Hot on their appearance in London, the splendid bound volumes had made landfall in boxed and girded quantity, already reprinted.

In January 1782, John Watt and James Stevenson, carriers in Irvine, had their carts unexpectedly stopped by Excise Agents in Glasgow. They were packed with new reprints, all illegal, all from Dublin: four copies each of Robertson's *A History of Scotland* in two volumes, *A History of Charles V* in three volumes, and *A History of America* in two. Under these, the Dublin printer had packed twenty-five contraband copies of Paton's Navigation, four prints of *A History of Modern Europe* and ten copies of *The Dictionary of The English Language* compiled by Samuel Johnson in 1755 and never out of print.

What a manifest of innocent titles, blameless education: just expensive and highly taxed.

They were internally addressed to William Templeton, Irvine, not intended for the counter of his shop, but for its cellar, a notable safe house on the careful quiet journey of smuggled books in Scotland. The bale holding these New Year's underground Dublin editions, seized in its canvas at Glasgow, was en route eventually for Robert Morrison and Sons, Perth.

Meantime, in the 'S' section of his Dictionaries travelling without passport deep inside the boxes, lay Johnson's last word on it all—

> *Smuggler: A Wretch who in defiance of justice and the laws*
> *imports goods contraband or without payment of customs.*

Templeton was fined in 1782, no worse, and his shop quickly opened again for daily custom, sales, and conversation.

What did he think, then, when later that same year, the

twenty-three year-old flax dresser Robert Burns crossed the High Street from the heckling shop in the Vennel and asked permission to look at the books on the shelves? Who did he see in the doorway and what did they say to each other—the recent smuggler-bookman, now town councillor,—and Burns, out for an hour from work in search of new minds? He was asking Templeton to let him look at prose, for rhyme, he said, except for some religious pieces, he had quite given up—though, he added, there were always ballads and songs to find...

It was a good time to discover the shop. Templeton had just begun to fill his walls with an ambitious sweep of new leisure books, a bold and modern enterprise he would develop for the next fifteen years. He lent Burns Samuel Richardson's *Pamela*, volumes one and three only, leaving him to fill in the plot of volume two which had disappeared. Did Templeton speak about the poets Burns had read in John Murdoch's schoolroom in Ayr? It's likely, for Burns admired them then, William Shenstone, Mark Akenside, Alexander Pope.

At some moment over those few weeks Templeton showed him into the corner where he kept issues of Ruddiman's Weekly and Burns found, for the first life-altering time, some published poems by Robert Fergusson, dead these eight years.

Why did Templeton lead him towards poetry? Had Burns confided some of his own work to him? Did he see here a young Scots workman ready to become a poet, and one as heady and driven as Fergusson himself? As passionate to write in his own language?

And did he have on a ready shelf the Thomas Walker *Romantic Poetry* volume of 1770—or even the copy of Fergusson's *Complete Poems* which he had ordered for his customer Benjamin Maul? Did he put that into Burns's hand too?

Was there a chair? Eighteenth century seaport town bookshop, ambitious owner, booklover—there would be a chair for Burns: and in this way the shop became a revelationary place in the quick of creation. Here Burns turned away from the English formalists and read poetry transcendent in the Scottish tongue and in the speeding rhythms of his own speech. He had come looking for 'ballads and songs', he told Dr John Moore in a letter on 4th August 1787, and he had 'found Fergusson'.

Having by this time quit the smuggling trade, Templeton had released himself from the risky company of brother booksellers still involved. He was now an active councillor for Irvine and by 1785 a shareholder in local coal mines. When he met Burns in 1782, he had just begun a long and unprecedented programme to supply local academies with unusual books: books with a difference. He and his bookshop quickened into the hub of an enterprise bringing imaginative literature into young lives. Children would not merely learn to read but to read with critical minds, following the brilliant vision of Benjamin Maul, schoolmaster in the town. Breaking sharply and angrily with the old concepts of books as manuals, Maul was opening out literature as an endless resource for living, not moralistic, not judgemental. Books were for creating a new self for the reader to be.

Templeton made his shop the source of these new ideas. He and Maul met in his back room to write their booklists for ordering. There had to be Penny-books for the youngest—small picture books 'for wonder and observation'. He bought in copies of *Three Hundred Animals* by Thomas Boreman printed for Richard Ware in 1730, 'a description of Beastes, Birds, Fishes with a particular account of the Whale Fishery, extracted out of the Best Authors especially to lure Children to Read'. He had some psalm books—but song books too—for singing together. Watt's *Catechism* was there and John Bunyan's *A Pilgrim's Progress* for the style, but also to give children images of paths, wayfaring, destinations in their lives, poetic journeying and arrival. He bought in a set of books to encourage handwriting not only for future employers to judge by, but first to give each child a personal signature.

Templeton lined up dramatic works too on the shelves—*Tragedys* and Playbooks for classes to perform: Oliver Goldsmith's essays, novels by Tobias Smollett and Henry Fielding. Thomas Pennant's *Tours of Scotland,* Anson's *Voyages, Robinson Crusoe, Gulliver's Travels,* he set out bright in the windows. He ordered in a cautious four copies of William Wallace in the Hamilton of Gilbertfield version from 1772, and sets of Scottish poets—James Thomson, Robert Fergusson and with music, Allan Ramsay's *The Gentle Shepherd.*

The long shelves, the high stacks, filled and crowded the shop on the High Street near the Tolbooth until 1797. New works were added as they appeared. Surely in 1786 he subscribed to Burns's *Poems Chiefly in The Scots Dialect* in The Kilmarnock Edition, ordering armfuls for his customers, and surely he must have brought in The Edinburgh Edition of the work in 1787. Did he tell every buyer in the shop that it all began there?

From 1789 he developed a new section of his shop to carry the innovative speculative mathematical stock he had gathered after becoming a subscriber to *The Practical Figurer, An Improved System of Arithmetic* by William Halbert, who had been in 1761 the number-wizard minister at Fenwick Church outside Kilmarnock. He and Templeton laid out their plans in the same bookshop space where Burns had read Fergusson, and where Benjamin Maul shared his vision of liberating children to themselves in books.

Halbert's *Arithmetical Journal* and the mathematics books on the carrel shelves were bought by Templeton first for schools but then, when they asked for them, he sold them to parents, men and women whose school 'counts' had deserted them in the fast industrial world of late eighteenth century lowland Scotland. It had been John Knox's sixteenth century dream that child and adult might learn together, and here, in this space-house of discovery, it was done, like so much else.

William Templeton died in 1797, some months only after Robert Burns.

7

SMITH'S BOOKSHOP
1 ANTIGUA STREET, EDINBURGH

7

The Lighted Stage

ROBERT LOUIS STEVENSON WAS HERE BEFORE ME. IN 1856 AGED FIVE HE CLIMBED THESE THREE STEPS FOR THE FIRST TIME into James Smith's bookshop at Number 1 Antigua Street, Edinburgh, and asked, in his child-Scots voice, to see the pictures. They were in the window, Sir. In the window and in his dreams, phantasms of air, cutlassed and pistol-armed. He called them 'Skeltery' after Skelt the original artist, supplier of flats, scenes, figures, scripts, and designer of imaginations. Beside them in the window, Louis could see a toy theatre to make out of thick card.

The place 'smelt of Bibles', said Louis, and it was wonderfully dark.

Number 1 Antigua Street had been home to books for many years. It was a fine end-of-the-street building on the eastern verge of the New Town, on the way, as Stevenson remembered with excitement, to the ships at Leith. It stood between the city and the sea with the sound of gulls at the door. In 1837 it was opened for trading by Mr Gray, a theological and classical bookman sharing the premises with Robert Ogle, Bookseller and Stationer, who then moved uptown to 49 South Bridge in 1840. James Smith arrived in 1841.

He was an entrepreneur with vision and ambition. He opened with books and stationery, perhaps making his start with Robert Ogle's old stock. By Stevenson's time, he had extended his window displays to show his new discovery—a toy theatre made of card, to be constructed at home, its stage fitted with bright scenery, offering a 'forest set', a 'combat', and thin metal slides to bring figures on-stage into the action. He also had the plays themselves, Louis says, 'tumbled one upon another'. He could not know that as he looked amazed at the Skelt theatre in 1856, the magical and still unsurpassable maestro of toy theatres was being born in London: Benjamin Pollock.

As the east end of the city grew busier, he was inviting in younger, different customers, children out with their parents. His window became a beautiful and colourful place to stop, where nursemaids like Stevenson's Alison Cunningham could rest a little. He opened out the shop with a circulating library, distributed stamps and soon was employing two young men assistants. When Stevenson was older, coming up to seven, and bringing friends in with him, those two 'demanded of us if we came with money or with empty hand', and treated them 'like banditti'. This was splendid: the whole elegant shop dissolved into a scene out of Skelt, brave young heroes standing firm against mighty and unjust antagonists. It would all break out again in *Treasure Island* and *Kidnapped*, on the deck of sailing ships, on Jacobite hillsides, inside evil derelictions in Edinburgh.

I first came to Number 1 Antigua Street as a student, wanting to stand in the shop and find Stevenson's books on sale. The steps were there, the doorway and the windows, though it had become a busy shop of another kind, stocked with newspapers and tobacco. It was easy to see where the books would have been along the shelved walls, and how the window could be set up for the theatre to catch the gaslight from the street lamp. The floor was just wide enough to be the stage where James Smith himself, perplexed into high words by Louis' slow quandariness, threw up his hands and shouted, 'I do not believe, child, that you are an intending purchaser at all!'

A century too late, I found no one there to tell me about the earlier books or their owners. The Scottish Book Trade Index has no record of James Smith here after 1879. In that same year Stevenson left for America. On 7th August he sailed from Greenock on The Devonia to join Frances Osbourne whom he loved, in California. Five years later in a memoir *A Penny Plain and Tuppence Coloured,* he wrote all that we know of his transforming adventures here in the shop in Antigua Street.

Something about his leaving Edinburgh in the very year James Smith closed his shop affects me. Smith would never know how mysteriously he had sifted and worked the threads of Stevenson's adult imagination. The magic effects of the Skelt plays and their theatre surrounded others too. For my seventh birthday I had them from my brother—the theatre was a Pollock one—who so irradiated them with the story of Stevenson in Edinburgh that this unknown city settled in me as a magic source beyond thinking. Later, the shop itself and the plays came to be a point of departure for me, a metaphor I could use for myself, one that brings together endings and beginnings, opened and dropped curtains, acts, scenes and denouements.

By 1960, Edinburgh was my home with husband and son. Like Louis' mother, Margaret Stevenson, I watched with a small boy as the trains puffed out into Princes Street Gardens, and saw him to school in the city. We bought books in George Street as they did and read them in the Old Town, a wonder-place spired and furled like the black etched drawings in our stories.

Edinburgh ceased to be my home in 1971, as it ended for Stevenson in 1879. It has seemed like exile to me, as to him, not to be there: as if another self is still there waiting out the time till the action resumes and the bright figures hurry on to the stage and into the story again. In the South Seas, Louis could hear the cries of birds circling the moorlands to the west of Edinburgh, over Hermiston. What I hear is the screech-slide of the top-gallant trams curving down the Mound and the fall of footsteps round Greyfriars on an early Sunday morning.

I went to Antigua Street once more, on an evening in 1984, the last day of a Stevenson conference at Salisbury Green. His biographer J. C. Furnas had closed the celebration with an envoi, his slow American voice addressing Louis who was clearly his longtime friend, just one not around to give us some updated words on that childhood, the journeys, the exile: and always, always the drifting dream of Edinburgh. Afterwards, away from the buzz and talking, Number 1 Antigua Street in the late sunshine stood back from me, as strange as a stage set. The corner stone was blacker now, more worn, the windows had blinds drawn for the next day's Sunday. But the gulls were there, and the long shining pavement running down to Leith.

The Skelt theatre sets transfigured Louis' world from static to what he named his Transpontus. He makes no explanation of his word, knowing quite well that if his reader understands, a gift of energies is exchanged. Such a transfiguration paints in a bridge between self and self, across time, and exile, and paradox. If it needs a source, a small black stone bookshop on a gull-blown corner, with a lighted stage in its window, is hopeful enough.

8

ATHOLL BROWSE BOOKSHOP
BLAIR ATHOLL

Stopping Place

THIS IS THE ONLY BOOKSHOP I THINK OF AS A PICTURE IN A FRAME. I HAVE TRIED APPROACHING IT IN MY MIND FROM THE NORTH but always it resolves into a quiet composition of shop, hills, road and trees seen from the south. How strange that should happen, because the Atholl Browse Bookshop was set in a lively place. Behind it fast trains from Edinburgh to Inverness drew in to a porter's cry of B-L-A-I-R Atholl! Its stone building had lived an earlier life as a petrol station by the roadside so that for decades, everything had swung in, stopped by, set off again. It was busy with transience. In 1988, it stilled into a bookshop.

8

The petrol pumps disappeared but someone thought to cover their trace with tall pots planted with flowers: and perhaps this swift transformation inspired the idea of green and white striped canopy blinds over the windows and the magical wooden book boxes (painted bright red) outside. This far north, place names petrify into winter sounds, Calvine, Dalwhinnie, the Lecht. Yet here at their edge was a sudden image of summer offering books and rest, with all pace slackened to a page's turn.

The new owners recorded how their first stock was gathered: a local minister arrived with boxes of Penguins, there were auction-room catches of books about fishing, eight boxes of fine Scottish books from a villager, countless works bought from a bookseller discharging his stock, and many ex-library volumes. They studied the locality. In a village quiet between autumn and spring, people would look for books on needlework, railways, summer fishing, recipes, fiction and the popular detective Penguins, the green ones.

I found this bookshop in the summer of 1991 on a journey to Findhorn to stay in the Community. Nervous and unable to picture the next week of my life there, I followed a diversion as distraction. Blair Atholl unfolded as a grey village with Blair Castle at the centre, a shining white long house in a green park with open gates. By the railway station a hotel more castellated than the Castle formed out like the opening shot of a film, its steps and great Victorian entrance chattery with summer visitors. And beyond, by itself, the Atholl Browse Bookshop. I pulled over.

The welcome inside was as good, as bright and unusual, as the French brilliance of its outside. A man greeted me at once and brought me coffee and we sat down by the window at a wide table covered in red cloth. The narrow aisles ended in boxes of books, the shelves were full, smartly new, and labelled. There were no steps, no disappearing stair, no big desk. Just books, all round, to search.

Almost at once I found *The Findlater Sisters: Friendship and Literature* by Eileen Mackenzie, the best study of two early twentieth century Scots novelists, Jane and Mary, urbane and witty women: and next to it *Crossriggs*, their best novel, published in 1908. Here is a modern woman character, Alex Hope, caught in a rural village (but always with trains to Edinburgh and Glasgow as escape). There are stretching choices, and none, until, with a deconstruction of her life, she finds a new way to take. Something in this book, Alex Hope herself perhaps, makes it a book for now—new bright-covered editions have appeared in 2009 and 2010. It's the book Jane Austen might have composed if left without family in Edwardian Perthshire.

When I paid at his table, the man asked me about my journey on. 'And how do I get back to the main road?' I had to ask, Findhorn now in my head. 'You don't have to go back', he told me. 'This road here will take you round.'

Outside I joined some customers looking at big bright paperbacks in the red-painted boxes. We were like the bees that were clamouring in his flowers.

In the next years, I returned three, four times. The stock was never predictable and never static. It came in from collectors who had eclectic minds (or large families, all readers) and Atholl Browse brought me *A Bullet in the Ballet* by Caryl Brahms and S.J. Simon, a rare collaboration of ballet critic and contract bridge genius, and their *No Bed For Bacon*, an inspirational ghost, perhaps, for the film *Shakespeare in Love*. I found *The Narrow Road to the Deep North* by Matsuo Basho, the thirteenth century visionary who surely became Robert Louis Stevenson in a later incarnation, writing and sleeping out under the pines, caught up again in their mysteries.

This was where I began to gather American Indian poetry with *Red Clay*, Linda Hogan's Chickasaw poems about her mother who veered between the gentle body-care she gave and the bitter words she spoke. Later there was *Talking Indian*, Anna Lee Walters' reflections on survival and writing, and her search for fourteenth century Pawnee Indian forebears, first on the Great Plains and then—where she found them—in nineteenth century reservations in Nebraska and Kansas.

Like a glittering playbill *A Hard Day's Night* lay on top of another book and I bought it to see how the Beatles made their film, and then the one it lay on: an Everyman paperback John Donne with a beautiful Doubleday New York bookmark among his early lyrics.

The shop passed to new owners in 2003. I've been back in my search for *Letters from Gourgonel* by Kenneth White. This trail bends me into the last alphabetical reaches of bookshop shelves, always at floor level and hard to read—W. B. Yeats takes me even further along. White is seldom there but where he would be, there is Walt Whitman, and so on Thursday 30th March 2006, my last visit, I bought the 1947 edition of *Leaves of Grass*, the Everyman 1961 reprint in dark teal cloth, for £3. The bookseller drew attention to some 'slight foxing on exposed edges' and I thought how his words evoked the wild forests assembled so near his books.

In spite of its twenty-year life, Atholl Browse always had for me a Scott Fitzgerald spirit of beautiful impermanence as if it would pack up and go overnight, overday, overmorning. It was too fragile, I thought, not grey enough, its clothes too much for summer, its bright face too young for survival. I was wrong.

Now in 2011, it is filled with beautiful art and design, and with flowers, and I think that may always have been its dream. The books, I hear, were moved to a bookshop in Pitlochry, near the railway station where they could still hear the trains.

9

THE GRAIL BOOKSHOP EDINBURGH

Saturdays

9

George Street. This wide straight eighteenth century boulevard runs between the vista stop of St Andrew's Square and The Royal Bank of Scotland to the east and Charlotte Square to the west, stone-perfect white and grey.

Mid-way along the street in the 1970s on its north side, a musical bookshop traded with scores rolled open in its windows, little cream busts of Mozart and Mendelssohn on tables, strung bows, a chest of woodwinds, a tasselled red programme. Posters for Usher Hall concerts—gleaming white curling sheets designed with Aeolian harps and old typefaces—decorated the door and hung languorously over gilded easels in the entrance.

Not far away, the most prosperous saleroom in the city took up a long and more anonymous frontage. These pavements were not now the walking place of David Hume and Adam Smith, but they were true to what twentieth century Edinburgh enjoyed: church-going, second-hand buying, money saving, and a just proportion of the arts. On many days a scouring wind whitened the stone and shook the green blind over Brown's bookshop, a wide emporium with a tearoom upstairs and a view of the southern face of the street and the generous arching elegance of The Assembly Rooms.

These were a perfect Georgian ideal from 1787 of balanced shape and solid foundation. Walter Scott dined there, Charles Dickens and William Thackeray stood at lecterns and read their new books to crowded salons. Levees swept through the double doors to dance in the great mirrored ballroom, figures curving and meeting for ever. Stylishly and with great good humour, the actor Alastair Sim danced with me there when I was eighteen, asking me what kind of University Rector I thought he'd make now that he'd been elected.

A few doors away, under a white and cream striped awning, a shop gleamed where my engagement ring was bought on a hot day in a later August, in a spell of time when The Assembly Rooms became The Edinburgh Festival Club, and I was there on the evening of that day, life running ahead in an epiphany of gold and brilliance. In the cloakroom, an elderly nun asked to see my ring and wished for me that my nets would be set in pleasant places. George Street was transfigured: even the plainstanes sang.

By the early 1970s when I discovered the Grail Bookshop at Number 26 nearby, I was beginning to need a perspective on all that living. It's hard to recall how I heard about it. The doorway hugged into a recessed little railed stair, five steps rising to a door of ideal proportions with a fanlight, eighteenth century wood and glass. A sheltering place.

What I heard and saw that first time was what I returned to again and again. The house it had earlier been had left its shape in a hallway, curving stair, and a room to the right where the books were. This was a New Town room of human scale. I had begun my Edinburgh life in a flat in Drummond Place, the middle floor of another New Town house built for balls and brilliant evenings, love and youth, the double doors to each room so ready to be thrown open on to candle-blaze and fiddle song that we could not go out to the kitchen without expecting to surprise a game of backgammon in an alcove. The Grail was different, a narrow house, intimate in scale, and it made the finest image of grace with intelligence that I had ever seen.

The books curved round in shelves against papered walls—pale red—and in short double-sided piers out into the room. This allowed for soft benches and single seats to be set within them for reading. The tall poetry shelves lay to the end of the space under a lamp. That was my best place, when I could have it, to read titles, to read poets. I bought Norman MacCaig's *Selected Poems* and read Ian Crichton Smith's writing for the first time: Philip Larkin and, just in, Seamus Heaney.

The Grail was a Bookshop within a context, the Grail Movement in Scotland, where the shamanic Mysteries of The Grail were transformed, with money, kindness and insight, into the miracle of changing lives that had given up hope. Between 1933 and the mid 1970s in centres opened by the Movement and through churches internationally, its members ran teaching groups, hostels, and the Ogilvy Training College at Polmont began in 1947. They became nationally known, and after the Second World War, increasingly international in reach. By 1962, they were ready to open The Grail Bookshop as an ecumenical place of new learning, interdenominational, aesthetic.

I knew nothing of that when I began this book. Confirming the shop address with me, an Edinburgh librarian suggested I write to The Scottish Catholic Archives in Drummond Place, whose Archivist sent me the history of the Grail Movement in Scotland and so gave me a new image of the Bookshop. My personal links with the Grail Legend were to Glastonbury, the Arthurian imagination, seers and quests, writings, books, forms of transfiguration different from the Movement's healing concepts: but part of a whole.

I see now that The Grail shop's purpose in Edinburgh was to lead an international dialogue through world literature. It was there I first read the thirteenth century Afghan poet Rumi, and Martin Luther King's speeches. I was led back to Christopher Fry's plays after years away, and started with Wallace Stevens and Emily Dickinson when I met an American volunteer working there.

The identity of The Grail Bookshop is still for me in its simply being there in the heart of Edinburgh, my town. Its second floor was open for meetings. Artists held shows, musicians came, poets read, play readings happened. One Saint Andrew's Night, Fionn MacColla read from *And The Cock Crew* his novel on the Scottish Clearances: Duncan MacRae performed. I missed them all, close-bound as I was to the books on the ground floor. With very little money, I bought when I could, and no one minded how long I read.

In the end, the shop closed in 1977, defeated chiefly by rising rents in George Street. I went there in no quest for The Holy Grail but I found something precious all the same. This bookshop gave me more than books. On a Saturday morning when I was sometimes alone, sometimes with my son, the brightness of its music (often Vivaldi), the conversations, paintings and soft quiet spaces to read in—and the way that all these were represented as good, and right—taught me to lose my habitual guilt that I loved them, and I call that a gift to have been given.

10

BOOKS OF WONDER
NEW YORK CITY

The Colour of Hudson Street

BOOKS OF WONDER WAS MY NEIGHBOUR FOR A TIME. EACH DAY THE TOWER BELL AT THE CHURCH OF SAINT LUKE IN THE FIELDS CHIMED on the hour, a green-red signal flicked cold and hot lights in a delicate green cage above the traffic, the sun crossed white on the sidewalk. What only I knew was that these were signposts to Wonder for me to follow: but first I had to leave behind the self I came with. I had to wait, turn round, look. What a beautiful place this is! Hudson Street, Greenwich Village, in the morning, summer 1992. Slim trees sidle the walks, one at each black gleaming door, the red brick houses are high-stepping and railed.

Black carriages could be arriving for evening balls and cards, Henry James is close. A big yellow NYC crane waves me on and I cross Hudson Street by the shine of a long silvery street lamp mysteriously lit at noon.

The handle on the red door of Books of Wonder was heavy gold. The floor lay boarded like a deck. Books were colouring the air all round, at my feet, above my head, round a ship of high white shelving careening in mid-stream. From inside, Hudson Street had become a glittering forest beyond the long window, where the bookseller was busy with papers. He was the only stranger in the room—everyone else I knew: Jim Hawkins, the Cowardly Lion, Alice, and Dorothy, Peter Pan, Tom Sawyer, Uncle Remus, and The Velveteen Rabbit. Rat, Mole and Badger looked up from opened pages of *The Wind in the Willows*, on the riverbank forever. High on a beam the Mad Hatter's banded hat tilted down, brilliant dark and velvet.

It helps to discover this shop when you have arrived at some question in your life. What's real? is a good one. Or Where's best to go now? Both were mine. Was it high time now to go over rainbows and through looking glasses? The shelves crowded me with worked and lived-through answers from writers in every culture and time, who sent their imaginations on journeys to search in places of the mind and soul—wayfarers in The Hundred Acre Wood, Narnia, Oz, down the Mississippi, into the clearings of German forests stilled with magic. Scottish writers struggling in personal half darkness had turned over their lives trying for the light of their childhood again—Robert Louis Stevenson, James Barrie, Kenneth Grahame, George MacDonald. They were all here.

On my way to arrive at noon, with St Luke's bell ringing, I had stopped by McNulty's Tea and Coffee Company in Christopher Street to sit at a table outside, one of the high ones, and read *Lunch Poems* by Frank O'Hara who was here in the Fifties and Sixties. He writes that it is 'Grace to be born and to live as variously as possible' and I think yes: there with the hot sun out, somebody putting orange flowers in a glass on a table, and a small-paned white-paint window by my side.

And now I was here in Books of Wonder. The room is surely square? Yet space is opening far out and moves like a carousel. I catch sight of Ichabod Crane, Anne of Green Gables, Curdie, Prince Caspian going by, a Mermaid and a Tinder Box, Long John Silver with Oliver Twist and Jiminy Cricket. At my back, in an endless frieze one of The Wild Things out of Sendak is dancing with The Tin Man and a Dragon. The white wooden stair curves by a comfortable corner to settle in—an enclave where a child sits apart, surrounded by open, shut, and waiting books. Dreams and quests have no national borders. Mark Twain is alive in Europe, C. S. Lewis in America, Lewis Carroll in South America. I wish a Mexican boy would tell me how he likes *The Cat in the Hat.*

On this day in Books of Wonder I wanted to be given an American book, one I had never seen or heard of, a New World book. When I asked him if this could be found for me, the bookman nodded, came down his three steps, ran his fingertips along spines and volumes, then handed me a slim broad-paged hardback in a dark red dust jacket, a beautiful book to hold: *The Mysteries of Harris Burdick* by Chris Van Allsburg.

'This could be the one you're looking for', he told me.

What I had bought with my $15.98 is a book made from mysteries, some drawings given to Van Allsburg as a bundle of enigmas, untraceable to an owner and baffling to the eye. Each one is finished in faint chiaroscuro grey and cream brushed to white. On every tall wide page, the images recess into shadow and at the same time resolve into a figure, a ship, two children, a boy by a stream, a bed in an empty room. On each facing page, the author has written a simple line of words, illuminating only in that the drawings seem to speak them.

They come with a deep strangeness, even a kind of humour, like dream encounters more comprehensible than life and almost explaining it. A boy stands against the skyline as a harp emerges from a stream.

So it's true, he thought. *It's really true.*

On the book's cover, four people are setting out on a journey by bogie-truck. The rail line is single, running along a sandbank on an empty plain. They have raised a sail full spread: far off turrets glimmer on a castle or a palace. One of the boys, half standing, has turned to look at them.

If there was an answer, he'd find it there.

No one closes this book unchanged for it releases dreams. Best of all, its readers want to tell a story too. Places are found, and voyages begun, landfalls made by people amazing themselves.

'Where did that come from?' they ask at the story's end, finding they have come very far from where they began.

Books of Wonder's own childhood years from 1980 were spent at 444 Hudson Street. Two years on, it moved to 464. By 1986 a sister shop opened its green doors on the corner of 7th Avenue and 18th Street, and in 1993, one year after I found it, the Hudson Street store closed the red door and all the inhabitants leapt and cavorted off to join the family store a street or two north. I've not seen it yet, but I hear that the newest Books of Wonder has grown up into a long wide paradise. In 2010, the owners promise 'to find you the best for the children you love'. Including you.

They sell first editions (and reprints of them) of Frank Baum's Oz stories and other early works, rare books bought by people who want to hold a lost copy again, or to read an early gift in the print and on the paper they remember.

A photograph of its doorway shows a shop-sign on a bracket. It looks to be made of dark green silk embroidered with—

BOOKS OF WONDER
Books for Children Young and Old

It must be made from metal or wood, I know. It's a chivalric blazon all the same, unfurls like a trumpet fall and opens out in other and further worlds.

II

THE TURL BOOKSHOP
OXFORD

If it were lost, then how?

IN OLD GUIDEBOOKS OF OXFORD SOME NAMES ARE NOT SO MUCH PRINTED AS INLAID — THE HIGH, MAGDALEN BRIDGE, CARFAX AND ISIS, BALLIOL, TRINITY —patterns of gold and blue banded with youth. Collegiate streets go heralded—Holywell, Saint Giles. Beyond them in the everyday town, the buses run on plain serviceable highways named for their destinations too, but differently: Cowley Road, the Iffley Road, the Botley Road.

The Broad and the High were named to guide the earliest travellers searching out their paths by dimension and shape. Between them runs The Turl named for 'tirl', an Anglo-Saxon gait, a strait place, narrow. Once it opened to a pathway from the city to Balliol and Trinity through the defences of the old wall. It is an allegory, a passage to be read in different ways, both a defence and an entry. Till 1363 it was Saint Mildred's Street and later Sylver Street for the gold and silver smiths who had their work cells there.

This is the street where at Number 3, The Turl Cash Bookshop stood, selling old books, maps and prints and a famously rich hoard of classic modern fiction. I came here first in the 1970s, scurried along by a friend in the last minutes of an Oxford dusk.

Ten years later, I was back, by morning daylight and there it was, this Bookshop, taller than I thought, three storeys and an attic under a steep sloping roof. Five stretching windows of twelve panes each and below them, the shop. A band across its windows carried the name—

TURL CASH BOOKSHOP — BOOKS AND PRINTS

The two wide shop windows rose high, the left one an open field of maps, a globe, charts, some folded, some stretched like sails: the right many-shelved and packed to the glass with leather-bound works gilt-named and bookmarked with ribbon. Like an afterthought of the glazier, a door opened narrowly down right, up one step, the entry loudly and harmoniously belled. At one time the pavement was too tight and the traffic too close for window gazing, but in 1985 the street closed to traffic and the old cobbled lane became a strolling place. The Turl Bookshop responded with piled up beautiful displays to be seen from across the street like a light-box.

I had been with strangers when I first came and the books held back. Now I began to make the kind of discoveries that come from travelling alone. The owner was an antiquarian by instinct and choice but preserved on a special range of bookcases the best of 1930s to 1960s paperback fiction in the Penguin orange and green liveries. I bought from him a 1954 *Zuleika Dobson* by Max Beerbohm, Philip Larkin's novel *A Girl In Winter* and *Brideshead Revisited* by Evelyn Waugh: C. P. Snow's *Strangers and Brothers* too.

The walls of the shop were shelved in dark polished wood at the Turl level, with a small central table and a cash till to the rear. Light filtered through to a stair with a right turn, short and thickly railed. The floor above shone down, the wide windows reflecting sunlight on maps, big white charts, pale blue seas and sanded shallows. The shining play between sky outside and those sea-road maps lit up T. E. Lawrence, Captain Robert Scott, Ernest Shackleton, and deepened the dark, dark blue star sheets of the heavens.

Joseph Parker was the first bookman to open up here in 1823 when there was a coffee house nearby to take your novel to, your new Walter Scott, or the last volume of Keats. With its long hospitality to books and serious readers, the Turl Bookshop was always a serious and varied place. I saw copies of John

Fletcher's plays there in modern reprints, that John Fletcher who was Shakespeare's friend and the brother-playwright of Francis Beaumont. Beside them, a long shelf carried smooth slim copies of poets: of W. B. Yeats, W. H. Auden, Louis MacNeice, Seamus Heaney. I wanted them all.

But my search when I was last in The Turl was for a green Penguin, long wanted and not found. If anywhere, then here. It was a slow day. I sat down on the little stair and looked about. The oak rail ran down by some shelves easing themselves into the wall: and I saw it, not suddenly, but just there by my hand, clear, green and white, black title and author: *The Moving Toyshop* by Edmund Crispin. My book.

It is a strange one with an odd narrative. Cadogan, a man in need of shelter on the Iffley Road, Oxford after dark, finds a toyshop with an unlocked door. Inside he discovers a crime, is himself struck down, and wakes some distance away. When he and the police return, there is no toyshop. A flourishing fully-stocked grocery is in the space, the sturdy grocer himself serving his customers on an ordinary day. Much later Cadogan finds the toyshop again, but in the Botley Road, on the far side of Oxford.

With his investigating friend Gervase Fen, a Professor of English Literature in Oxford, he solves the wide impossibilities of disappearing reality, in company with Jane Austen's thoughts, and Edward Lear's. By the end we see how it all happened, and wish then we could be baffled again and believe in the miracles: as we had done. A person reading this book in a room in Oxford can go out into the very streets of the mystery, where the puzzle is, and walk them. We can map them as plainly as the gleaming charts in The Turl Bookshop's upstairs room.

The concept of Mutabilitie is no stranger to Oxford and in *The Moving Toyshop* all is change and uncertainties. The book's author himself had two names. He was Robert Bruce Montgomery, author and composer, and he was Edmund Crispin, author, who believed in wit, in the interstices of the mind, in the mystery of books. He did his best work when he was all but solitary in Devon between 1945 and 1953. In the mornings he held fast-paced conversations with his characters, challenging them to dialogues. He lived in the mind of Gervase Fen, his intellectual detective, untangling toyshop from grocery, emptiness from death. He took the title of his book from Alexander Pope's line in *The Rape of the Lock* about the 'moving toyshop of their heart' and made it mean our touching longings for other and stranger homes, and his own need to imagine something better than what is, to turn mutability into a heady hope for otherness and mystery.

Writers have seen Oxford as perpetually a key to mystery: a turl is a gate to open in a wall. Perhaps this gift comes from the martyrdoms—Nicholas Ridley, Thomas Cranmer believing in light against every horrific danger of pain and death. The Colleges eternally promise newness—youth, the river, the punts, the sunlight, doors unlocking: the potency of their courtyards, those gates with vistas beyond. Philip Pullman set 'His Dark Materials' here, C. S. Lewis conceived Narnia. In Pullman's *Lyra's Oxford*, Lyra learns how to be free and find a road, how to loosen gates between the ironworks and the canal path. This is the Ox Ford, the crossing place.

The bookseller in The Turl Cash Bookshop put my book into a shiny white paper bag, printed with a medieval black-cut of his shop, his name and his sign: Antiquarian Books, Maps and Prints. I made it into a cover for *The Moving Toyshop*. It's still perfect and still on my book, years and years into the future.

Number 3 The Turl now houses a shop called Scriptum. Downstairs are fine papers, kinsmen to books, beautiful European parchments and exquisite handcraftings in leather journals. Above, up that short strong stair, the original bright chart-room is now a Classics Bookshop, and right in this place. Once I believed it was a room where I might find Prospero's Books, such masterdreams as *The Alchemies Observed* or *A Text of Music To Sail A Ship By* and *A Possibility of Earth in A Time of Stars*. I hoped they might be preserved in this good place.

They cannot be. But their brothers in art are there—masks of ancient and incandescent beauty from Venice, Renaissance voices heard again in The Turl.

12

THOMAS DAVIES'S BOOKSHOP
8 RUSSELL STREET, COVENT GARDEN
1763

The Actor, his Bookshop, Samuel Johnson & James Boswell

HE WAS JUST FIFTY WHEN HE OPENED HIS BOOKSHOP AT 8 RUSSELL STREET, COVENT GARDEN IN A NEW BUILDING, with a front selling room and a back parlour for conversations and discussions. Russell Street connected Covent Garden with Drury Lane.

It had been created in 1634 and was named for its ground landlords, the Russells, Earls of Bedford. By 1720, it was 'a fine broad street' and by 1762, when he began, it was busy with custom. The house at No.8 had been erected with two others between 1759 and 1760 to form a terrace. Tom Davies could not afford to buy the freehold. As he told his friend the actor David Garrick, it had been set at £1,100, but his long lease held and he would trade as a bookseller and live in this house till he died in 1785. It was simply designed with a basement and four narrow storeys of plain plum-coloured brick. Inside there was bookshop space, and a beautiful balustraded and panelled stair curved upwards to the floors where he and Lucy Davies would live.

We need to trace his eventful journey here. In 1729 he entered Edinburgh University, leaving in 1730. Was he Scots—surely his later friend James Boswell would have told us if he had met a fellow countryman? The strong person who emerges early is mercurial and reckless. He becomes an actor distinguished in his dashing debonair roles for half his lifetime. Then in 1762 he settles into London bookselling forever, and in that work, plays the most dramatic part of his life.

He disappears from Edinburgh in 1730 but by 1736 is in London acting with a company at The Haymarket Theatre. He played Young Wilmot in George Lillo's play *Fatal Curiosity*, an audience favourite produced by Henry Fielding, later the writer of *Tom Jones*, a great picaresque work reflecting by chance Davies's own headlong course into his twenties. His acting was well reviewed at The Haymarket, but we lose him again for a year or two until, as an anonymous friend said, he 'commenced bookseller', his first try at the trade, early in the 1740s.

He set up in Duke's Court opposite St Martin's in the

Fields and then opened in Round Court off the Strand. For over a century the book trade had been expanding, moving from Saint Paul's Churchyard into Paternoster Row and then west to Drury Lane and the Strand, creating a hereditary ground base for the bookshop neighbourhood of Charing Cross Road and Cecil Court.

Round Court was already busy in the 1740s with specialist map and atlas booksellers. Was Tom Davies one of them? More likely he was in general business with literature. There was so much poetry to sell: Alexander Pope had been publishing every year for a decade since 1730, and there was exciting innovative prose. Jonathan Swift's *Gulliver's Travels* had been out since 1726, Daniel Defoe was selling well, and now there was a new genre in the first appearance of the novelist Samuel Richardson, David Hume's Essays, and quick-to-sell copies of *The Gentlemen's Magazine* with pieces from young Samuel Johnson making his name. By the late summer of 1749 though, the book to buy was *Tom Jones*. Trade was whirling at the counters of Round Court.

But by then, Tom Davies had left the book trade, leaving no trace. Somewhere between 1746 and 1747 he had 'met with misfortunes' and had gone back to the theatre and to Scotland. In 1749 he was acting at The Concert Hall and The New Concert Hall in Edinburgh. He was now thirty-seven years old.

Edinburgh was popular with touring companies. The audiences were sophisticated enough for light drama and the elegant-reckless roles Tom Davies played thrillingly. He was retained in the company for a long tour to Dublin, to appear at The Green Room Theatre under the direction of Samuel Foote, whom he would meet again further into his life, in his Russell Street Bookshop. One other fact: the Company returned to England to play in The New Theatre, York and there he met Lucy Yarrow, the daughter of a theatrical family, and a supreme beauty. By the time he is again playing in Edinburgh, he and Lucy are married.

In January 1750 in a bitter Edinburgh winter, he is Edgar in *King Lear* playing at The Concert Hall off the Canongate near Playhouse Close. This old theatre cannot hold the new audiences and is in desperate need of repair: foundations for a new one are already laid but it is being built on credit. The January performance is to bring in money to pay the builders enough to continue. The Caledonian Mercury put it like this:

'By particular desire, in order to pay part of the expense of erecting the New Concert Hall, at The Concert Hall in the Canongate on 23rd January 1750 will be performed a Concert of Musick. After the first part of the Concert will be presented *The True and Ancient History of King Lear and His Three Daughters* by Shakespear.'

Two days later Davies was in *The Fair Penitent* and then he appeared in six roles in a hectic seven weeks: on 13th February in *Venice Preserved*, 15th February The Ghost in *Hamlet*, 22nd February, Manly in *The Provok'd Husband*, 1st March in Shakespeare's *Henry IV*:

29th March the title part in Joseph Addison's *Cato*, and by 7th April, he was (surely a weary) Osric in *Hamlet*.

In the month that followed, there were changes in the Company. Tom Davies's reputation was high and he was playing major roles. On 5th May he was given the title role of *Othello*. This was a benefit performance for him and has all the appearance of an accolade for the Company's new leading actor. In September he becomes Co-Director of The New Concert Hall. The Caledonian Mercury reports that he has purchased from the Proprietors of The New Concert Hall 'all their right, title and interest, together with cloathes, scenes, and everything else thereunto belonging'.

The New Concert Hall opened magnificently on 5th November 1750. Two days later, Tom Davies plays Horatio to Mrs Lucy Davies's Callista in the trusted *The Fair Penitent*, her first performance in Edinburgh. By 28th November, Davies is playing Hamlet. A month later, on 3rd December 1750, he and Lucy appear together as Othello and Desdemona, setting out on the partnership they will continue in London at the Drury Lane Theatre.

The Edinburgh Company continued their regular performances in The New Concert Hall through 1751. From then till 11th June 1752, when a guest-actor from Drury Lane played Hamlet, there is no record of them, and Tom Davies's directorship of The New Concert Hall seems to have ended. The *Annals of the Edinburgh Stage* refers to the unexpected cost of 'an enlarged orchestra, the special charges for a harpsichord and player to accompany voices, the payments to guest actors and singers from Dublin and London.'

But by 1753 Thomas and Lucy Davies are back in London, successful touring actors. They appear together season after season at Drury Lane until, it was said, indifferent reviews and then some low sarcasm from Charles Churchill in *The Rosciad* began to weaken Davies's nerve. After ten years on the stage, he became a bookseller again.

And that is why in 1762, he and Lucy are opening at 8 Russell Street, Covent Garden. The sight of a new double-fronted bookshop, and the gossip news about an exquisite wife and a lively companionable actor/bookman, brought Davies the customers he needed to begin. He never fully ceased to be an actor: the shop turned him into an impresario.

Here was an empty stage waiting to be scene-set into whatever his imagination and personal spirit would make it. He began to stock whatever was new—unusual maps, diaries, histories of military campaigns with intricate detailed battle-lines to be fought out again on drawing room tables. In July 1762 he bought three copies of Machiavelli's *Essays* for 12s. from George Hawkins, his wholesaler.

He stocked up with medical treatises: books on inoculation, histories of surgery, Thompson on Gout. Some were his own interests—the books on elixirs, the memoirs, history, letters, scripts of plays, Thomas Percy's *Reliques of English Poetry*. He bought histories of great estates and so made contact with families who might have libraries to sell. He bid for sermons in conversations with divines who became customers in his shop, and then friends through the talk in the back room. He sold novels in this enduring time of English novelists: Laurence Sterne, Samuel Richardson, Tobias Smollett, and Henry Fielding, his friend from the Edinburgh acting days.

His name and Lucy's were known to theatregoers and—a great good fortune—to David Garrick, the most popular actor of the time whose god-like presence in the bookshop ensured that others followed.

The windows were recessed and floored, allowing Davies to dress them with displays. In this time before colourful dust jackets, the window books were opened at interesting pages, illustrations, maps, portraits, cartoons: and sometimes at their end papers to show the gilt leaves, the vellum covers on the boards, the perfect cut of the pages. Where these were uncut, the book depended on the flair of its binding, its leather, calf and Morocco, and the brilliant clarity of the gilded title.

After just a single year, Davies could on an ordinary day look forward to seeing in his shop Oliver Goldsmith, Ambrose Phillips the poet, Richard Sheridan, James Boswell (who addressed him as 'Mr Davies, the Actor' in his correspondence, with great deference), and Samuel Johnson. If Johnson had heard that Tom was a consummate mimic of him, he decided to know nothing about it. There was a special sympathy between them. When Johnson's father, Michael, was a bookseller in Lichfield, his son had seen the suffering caused by failing custom, broken orders, lost money, the fickleness of the trade: and they were of an age, Johnson 53 when they met, and Davies 50.

James Boswell was less frequently present. He was in love with London but he could be there only when the vacations released him from the Edinburgh law studies enforced by his father, Lord Auchinleck, a High Court Judge. In the early summer of 1763, he came swift by coach, eager—no, desperate—to meet Samuel Johnson. To hear such a man would be to find a way into a new perception of the world. He was only 23, fretful already at lost time, sensing genius, wild to be away from home, longing to know Johnson, to watch him think. Tom Davies had promised to set up a meeting.

On 16th May 1763 at almost seven in the evening, when Boswell was taking a dish of tea with Davies and Mrs Davies in the inner room, there was a flurry of sound in the shop. Davies rose, pointed forward through the glass door to the shop and said, 'Look, my lord, it comes!'

An actor's line, out of Hamlet. It had Boswell on his feet. Johnson came hurriedly through, later than usual, catching sight of Boswell at once. Davies introduced him as having come from Scotland, gleefully pushing Johnson into his habitual attack on the

Scots, directed now at young Boswell who was 'stunned by this stroke' but not defeated by it.

What did each of them see? Boswell a little overdressed, plump-faced, watchful: Johnson, thirty years older, is bold and famous, instantly able to read fakery in a man but eager to admit a new intelligence. They talked together for three hours.

The friendship begun that night ended only with Johnson's death in 1784. When the great and truthfully titled *The Life of Samuel Johnson* by James Boswell was finished and ready for sale in 1790, Boswell held back its appearance until 16th May 1791, to let it be published on the 28th anniversary of that meeting. Although they spent only 270 days together in all, *The Life* is the finest evidence we have that one man may communicate truthfully and objectively the mind and self of another. Nothing else I can name is such a record absolute of two minds so different, and so engaged with each other, that each of them now stands as illuminated as when they were alive. Neither man had any glimpse of how these things would come about, but a few days after those hours in Davies's bookshop, Boswell was visiting Johnson at home and the great listening conversations had begun.

Meantime Tom Davies had books to sell. Competition for trade was quickening in Covent Garden. Francis Noble's Circulating Library in nearby King Street had begun to offer 'ready money' for 'any parcel of books'. More spacious establishments appeared, selling books and also art—Alexander Donaldson's at the corner of Arundel Street off the Strand, Jonathan Kendal and Alexander Hogg in Paternoster Row. At 8 Russell Street, it was time for the owner to diversify his activities, or in the words of his time, to 'find a competence' in writing and publishing.

Over the next fifteen years, Davies wrote, published and sold countless topical pamphlets, edited the Works of the seventeenth century poet Thomas Browne in three volumes in 1772 and the Poems of John Davies in 1773. In that same year he brought out *Miscellaneous and Fugitive Pieces by the Author of The Rambler,* who was Johnson.

By 1775 The Royal Academy appointed him official Bookseller and when The Academy's first President, Joshua Reynolds, inscribed his initial Address to David Garrick, the historic work was 'printed for Thomas Davies'. He had it made in quarto size with marbled endpapers, the pages uncut, the whole book laid into a half blue morocco case. Later that year he wrote and published *The Works of George Lillo with An Account of His Life,* a graceful compliment to 1736 when he was twenty-four and played in Lillo's plays at The Haymarket Theatre, in another life.

In 1777 he contributed a second profound service to literature. Early that year, he had received word of a new Collection of Poets being prepared in Edinburgh, to be sold in London. Its compass seemed to him 'small in size and print, a poor publication'. Therefore, following his instincts and speculating without money to back them, he and two brother booksellers quickly 'treated on a bargain' with Samuel Johnson to undertake a great new work. His commission was to write critical prefaces and biographical accounts of the English Poets suitable to be set within proposed new editions of the poets' works. Johnson agreed.

He worked without notes and needed no research. He wrote for three years out of his knowledge, the thinking he had done, his habitual reading and memorising of poems over a lifetime, and best of all, from his understanding of men and writing. It was finished in 1781, so magnificently developed with critical insight that it was published in its own right as a collection of defining essays on the poets. *The Lives of the Poets* was recognised at once as a summation and a future source.

Davies was struggling to sustain his own literary reputation while also administering his business. As a topical work, he wrote in 1777 a series of literary portraits of King George III, Queen Caroline, Sir Robert Walpole, Mr Fox and Mr Pitt, his first and only political writing. But increasingly, his situation in a crowded profession was too fragile. In 1778 he 'unfortunately failed in his circumstances' and was saved from ruin by his friends. Within days of hearing of the losses, Johnson, Boswell and Garrick persuaded Richard Sheridan to put on a benefit play for him at Drury Lane Theatre. The fund helped to restore balance and some confidence to him, and when in 1779 David Garrick died, he began to write what would be his own great work, the two-volume *Life of David Garrick*. It was published in 1780, was sold in his own shop and over the counters of his neighbours and rivals, successful and acclaimed by them.

In December 1784, Samuel Johnson died and was buried in Westminster Abbey near to David Garrick. They had travelled together from Lichfield to London in 1737 as young men, Garrick then Johnson's student.

Now, in the back room they had both known so well, Tom Davies turned in his mind to the theatre again to write his *Dramatic Miscellanies of Shakespeare.* His heart was still an actor's: he joyfully brought out a second edition only days before he died on the 5th May 1785.

On the 200th anniversary of Samuel Johnson's death, English Heritage assigned a Blue Plaque to Thomas Davies's house and shop in Covent Garden.

In this house owned by Thomas Davies, Bookseller
Dr Samuel Johnson met James Boswell
For the First Time in 1763.

There was so much more to say.

THE ACTOR, HIS BOOKSHOP, SAMUEL JOHNSON & JAMES BOSWELL

13

WATKINS BOOKSHOP
CECIL COURT, LONDON

Through

IT WAS EARLY MORNING. THE CAB DRIVER WARNED ME THERE'D BE 'NOTHING DOING YET' BUT HERE I WAS IN THE QUIET OF 10.00 A.M. OUTSIDE Marchpane in Cecil Court which lies between Charing Cross Road and St Martin's Lane, thoroughfares whirling with traffic and people, but here only a pigeon or two. This must be the best time to arrive.

Marchpane at 16 sells books for children and has curling ivy in the window. It makes a secret garden, a bosky place over-running the back panels. A heavy brown leather-bound Harry Potter—*The Order of The Phoenix*—stands tall among nineteenth century Alices in Wonderland. So many editions are there, so many illustrators. Yet every Alice is long-haired, fair, a young Virginia Woolf, pinafored, looking upward, gesturing with long pale arms and vanishing now like The Cheshire Cat himself on these old book boards. Behind her, balanced without holds, there's a poster in Aubrey Beardsley style, clearly an original even in the dusk of the window. It shows a fin de siecle Hamlet-young man elegantly buying books from a Wizard with a stall, a very old man, a learned Lear, a bookseller.

The glass door has 'Closed' on it. In front and nearer to me, hangs a folding iron gate, its two parts crazily, beautifully, unequal and unmatched. Where else would you see two halves of an intricately patterned screen from two different smiths? But how right—surely this is some fine solution reached in a corner of forested Europe, a dangerous moment passing as a wise man stands forward to the angry iron-masters in the Forge and says—

From both we'll take and make the gate so of each and both.

And here it is.

In window by window along the Court, I see early letters folded into packets addressed in pale brown inks, then sealed in gloss scarlet wax, stamped but not with postage stamps. Ink bottles, blotting sands. An unlit window is filled with glass bottles in green, dark amber, cornflower, aqua, purple: one is the cobalt blue of an apothecary poison flask. I try to see if its surface has quilting or spiking, protective devices legally imposed against error. They are of ribbed, plain, clouded glass stoppered baroquely, one with a marble for its top. Plain jaunty stoneware for early beer drinkers lie on their sides.

Another window has little toy theatres and figures. I have seen some in Edinburgh but here these are drawing-room characters, suave villains and beauteous women, more modern than the pirates in the northern shops. Streets outside the Court are named for the actors Henry Irving and David Garrick: Wyndham's Theatre and the Shaftesbury Avenue playhouse district are within call of these tiny audiences painted in rows. I'd like to see this toyshop window lit as it will be soon. Just now it seems as if the little coloured theatres have gone dark.

Here and there, though, inside the shops along the passage way, tiny lights like stars blink from ceilings, night-lights in the full morning, like Bethlehem at dawn. These shine on some wonders that have little light themselves. How pale the rarest stamps are, fading green and brown, and penny puce. The wide pictorials are from South America, glamorous queens, singers, women out of history, tacked now into place on silk padded boards, gold edged leaves. How Egyptian the Penny Black looks! Coins, however rich and old, are disappointingly unlike the doubloons and treasure in books—dazzling gold beyond belief. These are dark, used, immensely coveted.

The Court where all these are was built out of fields in the late 1600s. Through that first life there were cheesemongers here, brandy-shops, the Ham pub, Eleanor Pickhaver's boiled beef house, Kendrick the Bootmaker. Two centuries on, wild, rundown, too often scarred by fires and poverty, it was cleared and rebuilt into these sturdy well set-up shops and flats in the late nineteenth century.

The earliest tenants were booksellers attracted by the solid frontages, relative quiet for browsers, good safe stockrooms, the nearness of hundreds of people at each end of the lane all day. Just as the bookmen at St Paul's Churchyard in 1600 had relied on professions in the neighbourhood for business, so Cecil Court looked to the nearby civil servants and legal officials to be readers with interests in literature, art, music, incunabula, and, especially, in collecting—coins, medals, stamps, maps, model railways...

In 1901 John Watkins opened his first shop at No.21. Along from him at No.16—now Marchpane—the Foyle brothers started up too in 1904, with assistance from John Watkins. Soon film distributors and publishers of film trade papers arrived to sell and to stock flammable film in the deep stone foundation rooms. In 1912, or just after, The Pioneer Film Company Ltd opened at No.27, advertising as ' house for up-to-date comedies'. For a time the street became 'Flicker Alley'. The Camera Club began in the last shop at the Charing Cross end, and The Photographic News had premises at No.9. I have heard that Cecil Court is the original of Diagon Alley and that Harry Potter bought his first wand in Watkins' Bookshop. I hope so, for the sake of the old film ghosts around.

Under The Sign of The Unicorn at No.7 the sellers published and sold books on graphic art, music, architecture, literature and The Unicorn Press was established in 1902. By 1914 the trade in the Court was chiefly bookselling and the senior, first-begun Bookshop, Watkins' at No.21, was advertising a new specialism in London—'all areas of the mind, body and spiritual literature'.

By 11.00 a.m. I have had coffee, and Watkins' Esoteric Bookshop is opening up as it has done here every weekday since 1901. Had I been here then and in the ensuing years, I might have waited with W. B. Yeats, himself a member of The Hermetic Order of the Golden Dawn, who shared with John Watkins a friendship of interests with Madame Helena Petrovna Blavatsky. Searching London in vain for esoteric writings in 1897, she persuaded John Watkins to create a means of selling books on metaphysical and spiritual questions in the Hermetic and Kabbalistic traditions, to take a chance on there being a public in London for mysticism and occultism. He agreed and began his business as John M. Watkins in 1897 at 26 Charing Cross Road simply by issuing a catalogue in his name. In 1901 the year of her death, he opened his shop at 21 Cecil Court. In 1947, his son Geoffrey extended the business to include No.19 next door.

The shops have changed their owners since 1984 when Geoffrey himself died, but the name has remained.

I think of all this as I go in and as I sit for a minute before searching the shelves. The big windows are separated from the shop by curtains in pale tea colours. Towards the back walls is an ordinary staff door made exotic to me by a white fall of linen. A tall Indian philosopher/seer beside me has already found his book. He stretches, resets his turban, and settles to read. Among the shelves are little tables with trays of stones, white, blue, black, magical to the hand. In small wall-cases, silk backed in white, are others, but they are more precious stones, set in silver rings. There are incense sticks lit and to buy, and delicate carved boxes, figures, carved flowers.

I have come for a book. I am vague about its title.

'It has 'honour' in it', I tell the young man, 'and it's in the Pagan Ethics Series'.

'I've seen it!' he says. 'I know I have—let me look—'

He hurries down a flight of stairs marked 'More Books' and then I hear him call up, 'Got it!' and he emerges, one hand raised with my book.

'How did you find it so fast?' I ask him.

'We were trying to classify it earlier. It's between Philosophy and Esoteric, Greek Classical and Eastern...'

He is about twenty-five, delighted because he has found my book and has a true bookman's answer for me. He keeps it by him while I go looking at the Food and Nutrition section to buy a paperback history of coffee. There is so much to see: books that document esoteric learning from early centuries to the twentyfirst century: books that teach Oriental and Indian philosophy, psychologies, Hermetic Arts. Every established religion is here, detailed, referenced: and the Folk religions, testaments from the Natural World and Folktales.

Books open on the tables show plans for future studies in Divination, Earth Awareness, the practices of Yoga: Consciousness, Alternative Medicine, Contemporary Spirituality. There is so much I like but have no way of understanding: the exquisite beads and chains, the glowing crystals, the fine silks, the secret societies' teachings. Nor do I search to understand them. I need to keep for myself wide spaces of not knowing, to believe that other visions exist, to know that they are there.

I leave with my two books and go to the other Watkins shop at No.19. Once a house stood here belonging to Jean Couzin, a barber, who gave lodgings to Leopold and Anna Mozart from April till August 1764, with their child Wolfgang new-arrived in England to give his first concerts in London. I think of him now, aged seven, his gifts as unfathomable as anything I might find in this bookshop. How to divine them, other than as beyond knowing? This is a perfect place to be aware of him.

For all the many explanations here in the teachings, there are as many books about faith beyond explication, authors debating reality and vision in the conditions of the modern world, spirituality and modern man, in terms that allow for mystery, dissociating reason.

On 23rd February 2010 Watkins announced the sudden end of trading, the closure of 19 and 21 Cecil Court. Baffled at this loss, I thought of an e-mail conversation I had from the shop in December 2009 about T. S. Eliot's interest in Gurdjieff's works. An assistant told me he could find 'no real oral history of this in the shop', but that Eliot did have an interest in the philosophies the shop covers, that his 1948 play *The Cocktail Party* shows Gurdjieff influence, and that he quotes from the *Upanishads* in *The Waste Land* and makes reference there to Madame Blavatsky. This is the kind of conversation he and I might have had in the shop, an exchange carrying knowledge lightly and easily, asserting nothing yet informed with possibilities.

When we learned that the shop was rescued (by its neighbour at No.10) and would re-open, I felt it had been recalled to life. 'Spirituality of London is not dead', said the new owner. Nor are Watkins 19 and 21, nor their name, which remains. The staff has returned and so have the customers, who came to the Re-opening Day on 13th March 2010 in crowds, and brought champagne, Yeats walking with Eliot, Helena Blavatsky with young Mozart, listening.

THROUGH

14

KING'S BOOKSHOP
CALLANDER

The Reading Garden

THIS IS A BOOKSHOP WITH MORE THAN ONE NAME, SPOKEN OF AS KING'S, AS DIEHARD PUBLISHING AND AS POETRY SCOTLAND because its owners are booksellers, publishers, and at the same time, sharp and generous critical editors for promising poets.

The shop is a performance hub, sometimes a refuge. No name is printed over the wide front windows, there being no short way to describe what happens here: but a sign hanging out from the door says 'BOOKS' and across one window span, in cursive script, 'Book Shop' and 'It's Why You Came Here!' I react spontaneously. How can they know? What's 'It'? Where's 'Here'?

A connection is struck. I go in already part of a conversation.

And then there may be no one there, or someone is writing at a table and does not look up or speak till I have turned away. I've learned the gentle purpose: once a woman hurried in while I was reading, asking as she came, 'Have you a book on how to make jam?' and the answer was swift—a quick reach forward into a shelf and a brief word, some explanations, a sense of a problem unravelling, payment and restored quiet. Here is an owner who reads her visitors and leases out time to the ones who need it, who want it in this place. She is Sally Evans.

It is a long room with more light than comes in at the window and the long-paned door. The shining round table reflects like a camera obscura on three walls of books, islands of travel books, children's books. A tower of many colours turns into Mairi Hedderwick's illustrations, Narnia, The Grinch and other Dr Seuss friends, Roald Dahl... I move along the fiction wall and find a doorway with sight of a garden on a hill beyond, like an illustration in a Book of Hours. My mind stretches back to Narnia behind me in the window curve. There seems no way for me to go from the bookroom up to the sunlit flowers, but there is: only not yet.

I ask about a copy of James MacPherson's *Ossian* and we search the top shelves of Gaelic poetry in translation, a rare specialist scholarship renowned in this shop. The book we bring down is too fine for me. It has been richly bound in leather, like its neighbours, by Ian King, co-owner of the shop, a master-binder with a studio next door. Now I see what makes those upper shelves glow from beneath like Renaissance textile.

All I need is a working paperback, a mere text of words, not worthy to be here in this company of editions. I find, though, the book I need about Shakespeare's London, and a Dublin-set Maeve Binchy good read for a friend: and then an unusual illustrated book named *The Bees,* written in *terza rima* mainly for children, by one of the owners. Learning about the facetted work of Sally Evans and Ian King is like passing from one room to another where each is devoted to a gifted task. Both are poets. I sense multiple possibilities in them and they are hospitable to strangers in a kind of stern fellowship I have not met before.

After some visits over a few years, I am asked if I would like to come to the September Weekend where poets read their work in the garden. This is the undiscovered country, the glimpsed place of my first time here. Now I was to go into it, granted entry by poetry like a woman in a fable. The actual experience was more human and splendid. The garden gleamed with orange red flowers in Pre-Raphaelite shadings and tall pale trees, and before we read, we were guests at lunch at a table laid just aside from one of the green paths

Poets vary. They carry their poems in brief cases, crushed into inside pockets, in folders of sweetest leather, in embroidered bags, in ring binders: and there are degrees of fussing, laying out, searching the pages. I see with love the weary reader unfolding his two A4 papers, the anxious reader clutching at a falling page, the eager and popular poet, clearly successful and known here, smilingly surprised when her turn arrives.

I think of Robert Henryson writing in pastoral gardens like this one, delighting in human diversity in fifteenth century Fife, and saddened at its travail: and I remember Robert Kirk who was minister at Aberfoyle not three miles from this poetry garden, writing *The Secret Commonwealth of Fauns, Elves, and Fairies* in 1658, disappearing from his world in 1692, and never found.

In the audience some listeners are attentive to the poems, some pull their chairs round, half-away, taking the furthest lie of hedge to sit by. The readings are in English and Gaelic, like the books in the shop. When a poet has read thrillingly there are natural silences. It may be that someone will reach down for his violin or a flute and open out the silence.

There is always coffee kindly offered and after the Readings everyone is invited to gather in the shop for conversation. We leave the garden. I follow the little passage but miss the door the others have gone through. Where I am has no 'Private' or 'Staff Only' instruction—that's not the style of this shop—but there's a softish haze to the light as if the books on the shelves have not yet come into their lives, or have left them. Most are venerable, but may be waiting to be bound and transformed.

When I'm back in the bookshop, its long room is a little less bright as the September day lengthens. Readers are exchanging details, even with me, so lately met. A surge of energy comes through the space and I remember the words on the window—'It's Why You Come Here' and there seems to be an answer now, though none I can share.

On my first time here, I stood outside to memorise the building from the street. Two houses made up the shop and bindery: sandstone walls, some plants along the pavement, a delicately carved bookshelf of paperbacks. A step rose up to a blue painted door beautifully glazed in bevelled glass, and two Scottish banners, a Saltire and a Lion, leaned together in the porch.

Today I see they are flying outside at the windows from high iron brackets. There is something heraldic here then, in the passion the owners have for Scottish poetry, in the way they deploy their lives to have it written, read and known in a Scottish pleasaunce healing to the spirit.

ne dimensions, the balance, the line. O desirable new world!

Though I had no way of knowing, the shop was a revealed andscape in my continuing journey. I crossed a border in its hreshold and the world showed me more.

My friend had come to buy *Autumn Journal* by Louis MacNeice, a late edition of the 1939 long poem which would build or us the next spell of our time. The shop was close to the Central Library where I studied alone each afternoon, down three flights f white-tiled stairs in the Commercial Room, so quiet because istant from the crowded work-tables of the main reading rooms ar above. Every day about four, my companion clicked open the brary wicket gate, and I and my books went with him to a café pposite Saint Giles Cathedral in the High Street. Over many days, e read to me there from *Autumn Journal*, taking Part IV—though barely understood this then—as his declaration of love to me.

It had nothing of the sweet sound and flow of my studied oems, my Elizabethans and Victorians but I knew it was truer, a real girl who was near enough me for her to be me.

So I give her this month and the next
Though the whole of my year should be hers who has rendered already
So many of its days intolerable or perplexed
But so many more so happy:
Who has left a scent on my life and left my walls
Dancing over and over with her shadow . . .

15

BAUERMEISTER'S BOOKSHOP EDINBURGH

Leaving

MY SUN POURED DOWN WITH A STEADY GOLD. I WAS EIGHTEEN AND STUDYING LITERATURE AT THE UNIVERSITY OF EDINBURGH and every day in a wide room at the top of Minto House in Chambers Street I looked up through a window into the sky. It roved into whiteness, empty, not waiting for me to fill it with life, but unmistakably life itself.

For the first time, I was listening to poetry spoken like music and reading conversations with Charles Lamb who, I found, had my brother's style and humour. I leaned into drama, concentrating my Scottish ear on Elizabethan blank verse. I found Christopher

Fry, saw *The Lady's Not For Burning* and learned Thomas Mendip's lines by heart. People offered opinions with an upward tilt asking for discussion, not the immediate submission I had been raised on. Very soon I knew what this was on these autumn sunlit mornings. This was happiness, a new thing. The window was all future and the present was perfect.

Each morning I left my home whose disappointments and fears were the only seriousness, its vitality persistent in doubts and judgements. The Edinburgh train travelled fast into sunlight and my scanned and rhyming coloured world. I was learning to trust enthusiasm and to speak readily about what pleased me. There had been glimpses earlier in talk with my much older brother who read to me from Patrick Campbell and Paul Jennings, pages in P. G. Wodehouse and K. R. G. Browne: who took me to Glasgow to hear John Gielgud as Hamlet, to the School of Art to look at shape in the Mackintosh chairs and panels, to see paintings by Courbet, Rembrandt, Dali, Millet, Turner, Degas in the galleries. He told me that ideas were the work part of thinking, gave me language to make sense of them, and talked me into what imagination was and what it could do. I understood metaphor before I understood love.

Now in my light-swept new life, I was found by a companion two years older. He sat with me, he took me to meet his friends, gave me a peopled place with himself as a sudden and constant gift. Over four years, he met me off the train each early morning

and saw me away on the 5.15 from Waverley at night all r
winter long and into spring. We parted for the long summ
ordered a suit from a tailor in Rose Street each June to
in August in time for the Festival, when he would return
holiday job in a London bookshop. In this way our s
time was no longer than the time it takes to make a sui

In our second year, he took me to a Bookshop
enclave opening like a sunflower among the elegant
the top of the Mound. In the walled precinct of Th
Scotland and The Assembly Hall of The Church of
its window sang with the colours of its foreign bo
the zinging yellow of French literature and Victor
books, the pure white of foreign essays, the scar
of political black-letter history, the wise blue of
novels, romans et poetiques: and some Irish poets
smooth lettering on dark brown covers under the v

This was Bauermeister's on the Mound. The s
owners were moving steadily south in Edinburgh, tr
in South Frederick Street and later to open on Georg
They carried few textbooks and no second-hand
wood panelling was old, the wooden floors too, bu
shone. I had never before seen books opened out
here were huge art portfolio books, Georgia O'Ke
Homer, Pierre Bonnard, Van Gough, Monet, Jack Yea
itself was almost all I longed for: so perfect, so

In the old café, up a spiral stair, and seated at a shaky table in the window, I looked into the square below, winter white and darkening, and listened to the words. The book cover was russet lettered in cream tall capitals. He read with his eyes only on the pages. The poet—the book—spoke but I heard it not as a text but a meditation of the real and present, our life.

When the clock on the Tron Church chimed five, we had to leave and run together down a hundred steps to Waverley Station for me to catch the 5.15 back to my other world. As our second year became our third, and then our fourth, he ceased to leave me at the ticket gate and came aboard the train, staying on as it left, travelling on his platform ticket till the collector came, and then we paid him. On days of long light, he made the journey back by return. In winter my family set another place at the table till it was time for the last train.

Our conversations and our recognition had MacNeice's best of words to hold them and we added to them with ease, increasing ease, and truthfulness always, seeing the grace of ourselves and widening that into knowing the grace of others.

So that if now alone
I must pursue this life, it will be not only
A drag from numbered stone to numbered stone
But a ladder of angels, river turning tidal

The magic transcript of those years was the Central Library, time with Bauermeister's bookshop poetry shelves, the café by Saint Giles.

Then, though long in that paradise, I sensed a different life ahead when we had to make plans for our future. There were impasses. I had covenanted to repay money to my elderly father and mother with two years' teaching but now there were the promises to my friend. The jobs we both had in prospect in London, his home, agonisingly waited. We had no skill or gift to settle choices when promises fight each other, obligation with love, reason with longing.

Both of us knew about mutabilitie, time's winged chariot, and I could hear Yeats's poem on the splintering choice between work and life. We could understand Hamlet's fight between conscience and need and that the readiness is all. None of those ideas had made us practical and I backed away in fear of error or recrimination. We had been made strong by knowledge but had no experience with negotiation. The long pilgrimage seemed to have led to no certainty of anything except powerful feeling and I mistrusted that. I was wrong, too young to know how swiftly it would have taken us on and through.

The four years dissolved on a crowded corner of Princes Street, a place alien to our Old Town readings, our Bauermeister's, our café and the library. The choice was put to me hard worded, then immediately softened by time to think it through.

But in the considering time, I remembered what I had seen from that early window, the gleaming sky unmistakably life and future still to be known, and we brought our time together to a close.

Bauermeister's made changes too. In 1966 it moved from the Mound to George IV Bridge and a spacious shop fronted with tall pillars and wide windows. It had the look of a classical Greek Library, light, airy, noble. The old cash register had travelled from the Mound and stood again in use on the desk. Now and then I went there with my schoolboy son and then we would go next door to the Milk Bar: and I would run for no more trains taking me away from my happiness. So I am glad to have known them, the people and events apparently withdrawn.

16

CARRAROE
CONNEMARA

Henry James at Home

THE VILLAGE OF CARRAROE IN CONNEMARA IS SENDING ME ON A CHASE AS I TRY NOW TO PUT TOMAS MACEOIN AND HIS GIFT INTO words about a single day. It should be a song in truth, a song of a chapter. The picture in my head now is all impressions of a high wind and sun. I see the road on the coast with no end, only curves like Tomas's silences.

He is a singer like no one else. At Mass in the church by the shore his voice shimmers upward in a sea-cry, the choir sound tumbling in waves beneath, and soars with the pain and thrill of living in this extremity where his fields have walls cut from the same stone as the road, his house, and the church. He is a Gaelic poet.

His house is behind us this bright day. Once it was narrow and in need, old in an ancient place and fallen. When it was almost too late to save, he would not betray it back into the ruins of its first stones but would find another way to go on living there. It could be given new walls built round the old, he said, and so it was.

Today he had made me tea in the new kitchen and we had sat for a while in silent amazement at change. But the tea tin was all but empty and the sugar was done, and the matches spent. I began with my pen and a paper, always writing to make things happen, and together we made 'an order' to take along the road to the shop. It had been the Post Office when Tomas was a child.

The grocer's radio was playing springy music. His name was Micheal O'Domhnaill and away from here he was a popular actor and a farmer too. His shop was the whitest place in the village, brilliant with ceiling lights over the shelves and his counter. Even the paper bags were white, a neat lift of them raised between the apples and the leeks: two punnets of good garden strawberries tilted on the HD ice-cream cabinet. Farming newsprint, cakes and bread left by the van from Galway, the makings of an afternoon's ease. Whiskey too, for the night time, and lemonade, glittery-clear American Cream Soda, tobacco, pens, cigarettes.

'We need tea, and—'Tomas said. It gathered on the counter, what he needed, the sugar, the matches, the tea, and it all went into a white bag. Tomas was turning now, not to the door but to the far end of the shop, leading me to follow him. Back there, what might have been a cupboard once, and was now an alcove, had been lovingly transformed into a wide, low bookcase, painted and dusted, well away with its back to the noise and the hurry of the counter. Its little wall enclosed it, gave it a difference.

One or two of its books were sea stories, some were novels for the tired evenings. There was a history of Ireland, some maps too, and a short line of classics, beautiful hardbacks, dust-jacketed in colours. In this country, in this west land, culture is natural, unforced, unseparated from the day's other needs. Tomas leaned forward and said, 'Is there one of them you would care for?'

I found *The Portrait of a Lady* by Henry James. It was a book I would care for, care to have and care for forever. Tomas was buying it from the shop for me, to mark something unusual in the day, the house renewed, the weather brilliant and alive, the sea wild but kindly, someone with him to fetch the tea, the sugar, and the matches for the fire.

In the evening of that day, we met again, this time in Hughes' Bar in Spiddal, a legendary pub for masters of traditional music and singing. The friends with me were from home, from Scotland. When the songs began and someone called for Tomas, he would not sing: too sad, or just as likely, too caught in the warmth of the craic, his friends, his drink, the sounds of our voices. When the evening ended, we all went in the summer dim to my rented summertime house near at hand where the craic could continue.

Men brought in their fiddles and accordions and laid them under their chairs. The fire was made up of turfs, scented like moorland and warming the lamplight. There was talking and playing and somebody had stories about the Aran Islands and John Synge.

Time passed, people stood up with a quiet word and went home, till there were only two or three people in the room. The turf in the grate fell into small flames, and Tomas began to sing softly in Gaelic 'She Moved Through The Fair'. There was no other sound anywhere. He sang the last haunted refrain into silence, said goodnight.

The room was cooling, with the sky lightening from the east, but I sat on. Tomas's book for me glimmering on the window sill was an immigrant from America. It lay here in Connemara where so many Irish men and women had dreamed of its country and a new life, Tomas's family among them. Its Boston author Henry James was himself the grandson of Irish emigrants to America in 1789, by descent a Cavan man.

In 1989, not long before the time I write of, Tomas published a volume of poems written in Gaelic with his sister, Mary Flaherty of Galway. There was talk of an English translation, but he refused, would not have it happen. It is one thing to have your house transformed into a new shape, to let the joiners and masons rework it. But your poetry, your book, is your true dwelling place, like your song. And so this poem is for Tomas, my song for the book he gave me from the shop.

DWELLING PLACE

For Tomas MacEoin

No, he said. They will not translate.

The old croft where his father sang
And mother danced
Had fallen.
Rain seeped and soaked and pooled
The boyhood hollow where he slept.
No, he said. They will not pull it down.
They built around, confined it in another stone
Until his windows darkened
In a rim of ancient house
Humble and outfaced.
He made no sign
But every day
Intent upon the real construction of his life
Defied the burial of his verse by eager men.
For they would tongue his words,
Groove them
With a different tool,
Alter the beam and lintel
Of his line and render it
Untrue . . .

Offer a daytime for a sunlit noon.
No, he said. They will not translate.

This wintertime
His house is watertight. No shift of stone
Allows a comma of the starlight in.
His words are safe
And broken in their surface
Perfectly.

17

KENNY'S BOOKSHOP GALWAY

How to be in Ireland

IT WAS ALWAYS THE STAIRCASE THAT MADE ME GO BACK, MEDIEVAL-PROFILE STEPS CLIMBING THROUGH FLOORS, CIRCLING THEM, INTENT on the reach upwards to the oldest and rarest books, the last footfall touching on a wrinkled patterned carpet. This top space was a wide room like a New York loft with south-west windows over an ancient track from Harbour to Cathedral, now the High Street. To the east it looked down into an empty Middle Street, a white-stone place where there is a paschal look in the air. Columbus passed along these streets in 1477.

In that topmost room there are small stools to sit on, one or two covered with reddish gold cloth. There's no strict alphabetical design in the bookshelves: these volumes are not minded to follow categories. What they understand is time and so they stand and lean among their contemporaries, friends some of them, enemies too. The most expensive and rarest are cosseted in clear film covers for their age and famousness, for their being by John Synge, James Joyce, W. B. Yeats, Oscar Wilde, Samuel Beckett, Brian Friel...

This is not where I could buy a list of books, but one or two I have. The last was *The Circus Animals' Desertion* about the late work of W. B. Yeats. I bought it for Yeats, of course, but as well for the author, Norman Jeffares who was once my tutor at Edinburgh University. How young we were then, both of us: he conducted his 9.00 a.m. tutorials (on the nineteeth century essayists) with his cat listening on his shoulder. On another morning in Kenny's, I found his unmatched 1988 biography *W. B. Yeats,* a life and a study which even after the recent millennial decade of biographies on Yeats, reads like the one Yeats would have called noble and clear. I discovered more in the loft room: *Yeats's Myth of Self* by David Wright, a 1987 Irish-published scholarly work, and an early copy of *December Bride,* the 1951 novel about rural Ulster by the Scots author Sam Hanna Bell. The loft had first editions of J.M. Synge, James Joyce, Augusta Gregory, Louis MacNeice, Elizabeth Bowen, and, slowly arriving, slim copies of the newer poets changing through their lives, Seamus Heaney,

John Montague, Michael Longley, Derek Mahon, Eavan Boland.

Maureen and Desmond Kenny began to sell books in 1940 just a year too late for Yeats to have bought from them. The earliest shop was a room in their first home, and the shop's history is the chronicle of themselves, their sons and daughters. By the time I was taken to it, the shop was in High Street, Galway and was advertising itself very inventively with a huge poster of a three-level building in a snow-storm of books, all colours, shining windows and brilliant shelves. It was just like that. It glowed on the street among starry-windowed neighbours, close to a fourteenth century carved stone tavern, The Quays, a place of intense crowded hospitality and warmth. Woven baskets hung at the shop-door, not to sell, but as a hope of plenty in a town anciently of basket makers. Everywhere inside I could feel this splendid excess, more books than I could ever read or choose from, more paintings, more cards, booklets, paper for writing books on, notebooks for everyday and journals for leather-bound gold-tooled satin-ribbon perfect days to come. It was easy to long for time, endless time, to sit somewhere out of the way and look: to read and buy and read and leave, and return. In summer the sun crushed in too: in winter the books settled into their shelveries and except at Christmas, it was then a peaceful place.

Mrs Kenny herself sat by a small table, ready to chat, answer questions, and eagerly show you a book you could not begin to buy but longed to see. For me it was an edition of Ulster legends,

The Tain, far beyond having, but here laid out for me, left with me on a side table, to look at, to be with for a while. She would be seventy in 1988, the year I first saw her, dressed in a brown jacket, her brown-white flowered skirt curving to the floor. She was all grace, an Irish woman with sons working beside her, a widow now in the shop she began with her young husband nearly fifty years before when there was only that little room in their house for a shop. Her husband Desmond sold from a stall at Galway Fair and travelled the countryside selling their books, buying more.

In time they added the art gallery beyond the bookshop, a strikingly light place for exhibitions: it opened out on to the white cloister of Middle Street. I recall a show of rugby action-paintings, collisions and swerves swirled into canvases in scarlet, green, yellow and black oil paint. At another time the space held tall white blocks, each with a bronze Cuchulainn or Fianna Warrior stark and poised in the white room.

There were medieval corners. Round to the left of the entrance, the floor curled under the old stair and formed a tiny chambre des livres, a little soft-angled place with cards on sale, book-plates: bookmarks silken, Samarkand and delicately corded: diaries, finds, trouvailles pocket-shaped and sized for gifts, little books on owls and hawks and unicorns.

The great stair was hung with drawings and photographs of all the master writers in Ireland, which is to say, in the world, who had come into the shop, and some who were alive too early to be here in person. There are hatted and thick-curled heads, splendid lofty faces, oblique glances, profiles, straightforward eyes, marvellous women. They climbed with me stage by stage to the first floor, to books on history revisited and retold, folklore, legends, poets early and modern, working in Irish and English, well known and lesser so—Francis Ledwige, Percy Field, alongside the great names: books on the magic West of Ireland—Tim Robinson on Connemara, John Synge on The Aran Islands. Writings on The Abbey Theatre in Dublin, and The Druid Players in Galway, plays by Oscar Wilde, Richard Sheridan, John Synge, Brian Friel, Frank McGuinness...

Winding behind these lay the fiction section with framed cartoons and elegantly-printed comments and quotations. Antiquarian maps too and historical charters—so much to see. Books for children—anthologies of poetry for them as well as fiction and learning books. Huge enchanting picture books painted by John Burningham, gardens of yellow and red: bazaars and souks of colour by Brian Wildsmith, Maurice Sendak, strange, reticent, unsettling colourings by Chris Van Allsburg. Some steps above the Children's Books, the stair rose into the Rare Book floor where we began. By now the photographs on the stair gallery were of modern writers, and in the loft room, recently photographed, my son as songwriter-poet-musician.

This room for rarest precious editions brought nearer the books I might hold but never possess, a sensation like the experience of faery dreamers with their lovers. But I have had my visions there: a first edition Yeats signed, an inscribed first edition Joyce. Was it there I saw a letter from Maud Gonne to Yeats? That may have been in Dublin, though, for there are other enchanted loft rooms where a book, a letter, is transfigured by time into a dream and changes into more than itself.

In September 2005, Kenny's moved from High Street, Galway to a site outside the city to become an on-line business. Desmond Kenny has lately begun a bookshop within their base, and started a Gallery there too with his family. Mrs Kenny died in 2007: her children carry on her name and the history she made.

I send for books, pay in silence on line: but the book comes in and is real then, though from whom or by whose hand, I can never know. It is legend of a different kind: a supplication and an answer.

18

ATLANTIS BOOKSHOP LONDON

A Light to Shine Before

PLATO'S MARINERS REMEMBERED ALL THEIR DAYS HOW THE ISLAND OF ATLANTIS SHONE, HOW THE TEMPLES WERE GARNISHED WITH SILVER pinnacled in gold, all ivory and gold within, and orichalcum, copper to gleam. Like all magical places it was rounded with trial and places of endeavour.

Landfall at The Atlantis Bookshop in Museum Street, London is also made after spells in spaces of transformation. First there is the map-shop *Imago Mundi* whose window is richly coloured with fifteenth and seventeenth century maps. We need to go close to study them. The seas are made of parchment and creatures. The land is all red sinews and muscle-mass, the human body realised as its world. There are shapes in the air on those maps whose earths are younger than ours, and we almost know them. What world do we travel in an ancient map? What language do we speak? Who are our children?

Across the street, the Cartoon Museum is featuring Heath Robinson. Like medieval puzzles, his labyrinths of string are drawn meticulously on white paper and play out slow transformations into vast and interweaving clarity and solutions, ways to be found through the knot work. He is Ariadne to our Theseus taking us through the maze. Nothing asserts here: everything evolves.

The British Museum nearby holds its invisible ancient powers and its Egyptian Hero gods within wide gardens as vista stop to this small street where half way along, I see the Atlantis Bookshop shining sea blue. Across the window are written OCCULT BOOKSHOP MAGIC and beyond the glass the lights are gold. I have made my landfall.

Just inside stands Thoth, the ibis-headed god who created himself through the power of language, of words: who invented writing and created magic, a same gift. He may be also Hermes, the messenger of the gods and their recorder. He may be the Questioner of the Dead who weighs the soul of each against a feather in a scale. He is speaker and writer. Today, colour streams on him from the books on the centre shelves. There is light from the ceiling, from sconces, from lamps, from gleaming picture-glass.

At the far wall a desk is weighted with papers and books docketed with markers. The owner is seated there. She is brightly dressed and smiling. What world is this I've found?

I have a commission to carry through—to buy some books for my son. One or two will be ordered: the others are here. I watch as they are found, a series from Tartarus Press, uniform in a livery of pale matt cream. They are long and slim and come to the desk like tablets from Byzantium. Beside me is a fireplace and above that an old, big, mirror hangs. The books on the mantelpiece are not deep, to match its width: a little journal, reflections on Angels, some poetry, three neat leather-bound travel books on Egypt.

The tables and shelves are rich in books about telling. Here are Myths, tales of Superstition, of dreams and visitations. Some elegant and diagrammed books on Magic stare outward like Arch Mages, some chunky volumes about Magic are tucked companionably along the shelf. *The Book of English Magic* is beautifully eerily northern and pale. What will be different about English Magic? I look at James Frazer's *The Golden Bough* in three editions, each cover alive with the artist's imagination, his own deep dreaming.

I'd like to have this copy of Dion Fortune's *Glastonbury, Avalon of The Heart* for in it she argues that Glastonbury is Avalon and that its surroundings, the drowned lands of Lyonesse, may be the lost kingdom of Atlantis. Here are works by Gerald Gardner and Aleister Crawley from the very earliest years of the shop.

Round a corner, I stop by a biography of Piotr Ouspensky, and a modern reading of the women's action reformer Annie Besant who was both a Fabian and President of the Theosophy Society, her writings attracting Allen Ginsberg and Jack Kerouac. There is a central interest in the Atlantis Bookshop in Madame Helena Petrovna Blavatsky the late nineteenth century Russian mystic whose framed photograph stands above my head. She was the intellectual and spiritual drive of most of the writers here.

In a corner I see an account of Francis Bacon and the sixteenth century Rosicrucians with behind it a vivid text on Freemasonry. Some visitors come to this bookshop simply to read titles from another dimension.

Alchemist/Philosophers from the seventeenth century are assembled together straight and definite in colour, their hazardous propositions barely tamed within the boards. I look for the thirteenth century magician Roger Bacon and more closely for Queen Elizabeth's mathematician Dr John Dee who had the largest library in England in his time. He defined his work by allowing no separations between his calculations and his magic. Both were 'pure verities' to him, proven truths powerfully to be discovered under the visible world and instrumental in it every day. His beliefs were for him expressed absolutely in the cosmographic harmonies of Leonardo's *Vitruvian Man*. He had seven copies.

T. S. Eliot must surely have bought some of his copies of Gurdjieff here. The shop was already open in 1922 (though not in

Museum Street) when he published 'Waste Land' and was still in search of the 'miraculous, the exercises in attention and observations' in Piotr Ouspensky. The shop came to Museum Street in 1946, just two years after his 'Four Quartets' appeared, documenting—like the history of Lost Atlantis itself perhaps—'passing moments in a single day and a night of misfortune'.

Leafy plants hanging over shelves are reflected and a little magnified in the mantel-mirror and a great unfamiliar bird flies there too from across the room. What is strange is never far from what is local and inviting. Notices of events are tagged to the wooden shelves and the walls detailing Workshops and Courses, Speakers, a Moot. Rural baskets white-linen lined, carry leaflets, tarot packs, cards and candles. No surface is plain. A carousel turns with cards exotically figured. Behind me on a lit table are book jackets covered with drawn astrolabes, stars and moons. Here is the full and always up-to-date stock of astrology books, the sacred texts, the Mysteries. These are big books—readers are given a chair to make opening them easier: a bound work on Celtic Alba which is Scotland, one on Celtic Shamanism and Celtic Myths, *Faeries in the Irish Tradition.*

This occult bookshop carries some fiction and general books. I buy a small book about Tarot, and then, looking out at Museum Street, I discover in the window display a small white table bearing a lit lamp. It seems like a potent and delicate last defence against the cold stone and morning.

There is no music playing and yet I've felt a rhythm in this big room: it's in my heart, perhaps, or in the life of the shop. A delivery has arrived and must be signed-for and set aside, but once the door closes, the room stills again to the sea fall-and-rise of itself.

My son's books are packed—it's time to go. At the desk I have too many books to carry away and so the beautiful tablets will be posted on. I hear the words of my home's address spoken out in this room, my earthly location in touch now with the magic here.

I think of where it must be on the maps in *Imago Mundi.*